It All Started in Brooklyn

My Treasured Memories of Growing Up in a Place Like No Other

TOM GRIPPA
Foreword by Brandon Steiner

Published by
Tom Grippa
MACUNGIE, PA

ISBN-13: 979-8-218-72391-0

Copyright © 2025 by Tom Grippa

All rights reserved. This book or any portion thereof may not be reproduced or used in any manner whatsoever without the express written permission of the publisher, except for the use of brief quotations embodied in critical articles or book reviews.

Edited by Carol Killman Rosenberg
www.carolkillmanrosenberg.com

Cover and interior design by Gary A. Rosenberg
www.thebookcouple.com

I dedicate this book to . . .

All the people I shared my Brooklyn experience with: my mother, Maria; my father, Biagio; and my older brother, Vincent, who's been the guiding light in my life.

My wife, Tina, who has been by my side for over forty-eight years, and my better half (legally speaking) for forty-five of those years. Tina has given me a beautiful life with a loving and caring family. My life changed for the better when she entered it.

My daughter and son, Elizabeth and Robert. I'm so proud of their professional and personal accomplishments. Watching them grow and develop over the years into the loving parents they have become has filled my heart with joy.

My grandchildren: Lila Marie, James Philip, and John Thomas. They are thirteen, ten, and six, respectively, as I write this book. Hopefully they learn a few things about crazy Grandpa and gain some life lessons in the process.

My in-laws who became my family: my mother-in-law, Annabelle; my father-in-law, Bertram; my brother-in-law, Alan; Alan's wife, Mairead; and my sister-in-law Nadine. In time, all of them figured out that this Sicilian kid from Brooklyn wasn't part of an organized crime family—some sooner than others. In the end, we all became *famiglia!*

My sister-in-law Sue, who became the sister I never had. She came into my life when I was only twelve years old and has been a big part of it ever since.

My son-in-law, Jason, the guy who married my little girl. We hit the jackpot with him! He's a loving husband and father to my grandchildren. He does it all. Plus, he makes my little girl a happy camper, which can be challenging at times.

The borough of Brooklyn and my extended family and friends. I wouldn't be *me* without you!

And, last, the Brooklyn vernacular that I acquired over the years.

Fuhgeddaboudit! Youse guys knows exactly what I'm tawkin' bout! We can discuss lateaa over a cuppa cawfee!

Of course, I don't think I speak anything like this. I left Brooklyn more than forty-five years ago. However, in my travels, strangers have stopped me after hearing me speak to say, "You're from Brooklyn, right?"

I guess you can leave Brooklyn, but Brooklyn never leaves you!

Contents

Foreword ix
Introduction 1

One	My Famiglia Comes to Boro Park	3
Two	My Pets	10
Three	Apartment Life	14
Four	The Block	18
Five	The Neighborhood	25
Six	My Extended *Famiglia*	32
Seven	Bye-Bye, Dodgers! Hello, Mets!	38
Eight	My Dad, the Dealmaker and TV Repairman	45
Nine	A Tree Falls in Brooklyn	51
Ten	The Holidays	54
Eleven	Coney Island	57
Twelve	Catholic School	61
Thirteen	Almost Jersey Bound	66
Fourteen	Meet the Beatles	69
Fifteen	Our New Home in Gravesend	71

Sixteen	The New Block(s)	76
Seventeen	The New Neighborhood	82
Eighteen	PS 215	90
Nineteen	After-School Activities	93
Twenty	The Schoolyard	96
Twenty-One	Strat-O-Matic Baseball	99
Twenty-Two	The Ouija Board	101
Twenty-Three	David A. Boody, JHS 228	104
Twenty-Four	Abraham Lincoln High School	109
Twenty-Five	Off to Cooperstown	115
Twenty-Six	Brooklyn Dudes	118
Twenty-Seven	Wildwood Days	122
Twenty-Eight	Borough of Manhattan Community College	124
Twenty-Nine	The Lottery and the Army National Guard	127
Thirty	The New Band	132
Thirty-One	Brooklyn College	135
Thirty-Two	College Road Trips	141
Thirty-Three	College Rides	148
Thirty-Four	Back at School	150
Thirty-Five	Transcendental Meditation (TM)	156
Thirty-Six	Time to Work	159
Thirty-Seven	Son of Sam	164
Thirty-Eight	The Blizzard of 1978	166

Thirty-Nine	Sheepshead Bay	168
Forty	Tying the Knot	171
Forty-One	Returning to our Brooklyn Roots	177
Forty-Two	My In-Laws Leave Brooklyn for Arizona	179
Forty-Three	The Brooklyn Honeymoon Was Over	183
Forty-Four	Finding My Faith Again	187
Forty-Five	Maintaining Brooklyn Friendships	190
Forty-Six	Brooklyn's Untold Benefits	192
Forty-Seven	Brooklyn's Famous	194
	Brooklyn's Famous Comedians	194
	Brooklyn's Famous Actors and Performers	195
	Brooklyn's Famous Athletes and Sports Figures	195
	Brooklyn's Famous Locations & Landmarks	196
	Brooklyn's Famous Foods, Desserts & Beverages	197
	Brooklyn's Famous Inventions	197
	Brooklyn's Famous Companies	197
	Brooklyn's Famous Accent	198
	Brooklyn's Famous Weather	198
Epilogue		199
Acknowledgments		201
My Photos		203
About the Author		227

Foreword

Growing up in Brooklyn, the schoolyard of PS 215 served as the central gathering place for our neighborhood, which consisted of both older and younger kids. Tom Grippa, a friend and one of the older members of our group, always looked out for us younger ones.

Brooklyn: a unique time and place where nicknames were common, everything was significant, and fun required little planning. This book explores an irreplaceable era in Brooklyn's history from fifty years ago, an experience that cannot be revisited.

Kids played freely, organized their own games in schoolyards, and impromptu teams formed on each block, ready to compete against the next. Neighbors looked out for each other's children, not hesitating to guide them. This strong sense of community and self-organized play defined our adolescence in Brooklyn during that time.

Brooklyn instilled in us the crucial skill of navigating diverse communities. As Tom Grippa explores in his book, the neighborhood was a melting pot of nationalities, ages, and backgrounds, fostering a unique collaborative environment. This upbringing, characterized by shared food, strong family values, religious diversity, and the simple joys of playing outdoors, shaped our formative years.

Our teachers further strengthened this sense of community by actively engaging beyond the classroom.

This book captures the distinctiveness and powerful community spirit of our upbringing. The stories within depict a time and place of such unique character that its replication seems impossible.

Tom's recollection of growing up in Brooklyn brought back many great memories for me. His stories about the neighborhood we grew up in were spot on. No, we probably won't witness that era again in our lifetime, but it was enjoyable going back in time, reading about the wonderful community where we spent our childhood.

—Brandon Steiner
Keynote Speaker / Author / CEO @The Steiner Agency
@starstock / Host of CX Live on @ebay
Host of "What's it Worth" on @espn
Founder @collectiblexchange / The Collector's Vault
with Brandon Steiner on Gotham Sports

Introduction

Brooklyn born and raised! This statement is often proclaimed with immense pride by those who hail from the borough. What contributes to Brooklyn's distinctiveness and the reverence it inspires? Is it the notable individuals who grew up there, its iconic landmarks and locations, its celebrated cuisine and beverages, its groundbreaking inventions, its renowned businesses, our characteristic accent, or even its weather? While I can't address all these questions (except perhaps the one about the weather), I will share my perspectives at the conclusion of this book.

In the meantime, I aim to offer my viewpoint and present intriguing details about the people, places, and experiences that shaped my time living in Brooklyn. This book isn't a historical account of Brooklyn, filled with dates or nostalgic images of iconic places. If that's what you were hoping for, you might be disappointed. However, before you set this book aside, consider sharing it with someone who might appreciate a different kind of Brooklyn story—a personal journey through the eyes of someone who lived and breathed its unique atmosphere. Within these pages, you'll find my individual experiences, the moments and encounters that shaped my life growing up in Brooklyn, a place like no other.

It's not a chronicle of landmarks, but a collection of memories, perspectives, and the distinct flavor of my Brooklyn upbringing. Throughout this book, I share the good, the bad, and the ugly of my twenty-seven years living there and subsequent years visiting. While I promise not to dwell on the unpleasant aspects of Brooklyn, it might be difficult to completely avoid them when discussing my sixth-grade Catholic school experiences. That is the only bad and ugly thing that I dedicated an entire chapter to in this book. Catholic school was just a small part of my early childhood experience, which although it was traumatic, it didn't define how I felt about growing up in Brooklyn. When I think back on my early years there, I have only fond and wonderful memories of my family, friends, and places I frequented. I hope you will find these memories amusing and relatable to your own childhood experiences. At the end of this book, I share some pictures that my dad, brother, and I took while living in Brooklyn.

Please remember, I am no historian, just a kid now seventy-two years young, who grew up in Brooklyn and wants to share his story with you. This story is unique to me but may trigger some memories for you. It may also mirror your childhood, even if you were born in Sheboygan, Hoboken, or anywhere else in our great country. I share my story in a humorous and sometimes twisted manner. Why would I do it that way? Because I think I have a good sense of humor (to be determined) and I definitely have a twisted mind (I've been told). It should be a fun and interesting journey that I hope you will enjoy.

If you just read my introduction and plan on putting this book back on the shelf, please give the first chapter a chance. You never know, you might like it, just like Mikey did in that cereal commercial, back in the seventies. Then you can pass it on to your friends and family members after reading the last page. Sharing is caring.

Please come along on my trip down memory lane, where it all started in Brooklyn.

CHAPTER ONE

My Famiglia Comes to Boro Park

Here's a little background on how my life journey began in Borough Park, Brooklyn. I will refer to it as Boro Park going forward, as that was the acceptable name used by everyone who lived there. My paternal grandfather first came to the United States in 1906. My maternal grandparents followed in 1910 and 1913. My paternal grandmother and father immigrated permanently in 1920, and my mother arrived in 1935. My grandmother and father settled in New York City, and my mother lived in Brooklyn. All four of my grandparents were born in Italy. When they arrived in America, they were processed at Ellis Island, the "Island of Hope." Several of my grandparents' siblings also immigrated through Ellis Island. While some settled in the New York City and Tri-State Area, over time, their descendants spread across the country. I have found relatives in New Jersey, Pennsylvania, Ohio, Massachusetts, New England, and California.

My parents, Biagio and Maria, were born in 1913 and 1920 in Francavilla di Sicilia. Sicily is a large island off the southernmost part of Italy. Francavilla is a province of Messina with a population of around four thousand.

Being from a small town where everyone seemed to know one another, not surprisingly their families were close friends. In fact, both my grandmothers were extremely close. Unbeknownst to my maternal grandmother as she cradled my infant father, he was destined to become her son-in-law. This family connection deepened when my father's aunt married my mother's uncle.

Despite immigrating to America at different times, my parents' shared heritage and principles fostered their union. They eventually married and settled in Boro Park, Brooklyn.

When they married in 1943, they lived on 54th Street off 18th Avenue. I assume that neighborhood was selected because their *"famiglia e paisanos"* all lived in that section of "Brook a lean." Actually, their married aunt and uncle lived just a few blocks away from them. They moved eight years later, with my six-year-old brother, Vincent, to an apartment on 58th Street and 14th Avenue. A year after that, I came into this world via Maimonides Hospital and would join them for the next twenty-seven years of my life in Brooklyn. This is how I landed in Boro Park instead of Beverly Hills.

Securing decent housing during the war years was very difficult. My parents were not content with their first apartment in Boro Park. They were living in an illegal two-family home with a shared front entrance. Every time they entered or exited that house, they had the pleasure of seeing their landlord sitting in his living room, hopefully not in his underwear.

Through the years they were always exploring their housing options. All their friends and family would be looking for better housing accommodations for them. When an apartment became available, common practice suggested paying a few bucks to the building superintendent (who was referred to as the super) to be placed at the top of the waiting list. After my father made his deposit with the super on 14th Avenue, he was awarded a three-room apartment, which included one bedroom, one bath, a kitchen, and a parlor. Yes, a parlor! Growing up in Brooklyn in those days, a living room was referred to as a parlor. I have no idea when a parlor transformed into a living room. As I said, I'm no historian.

Did I mention that this prime location they found was on the top floor of a four-story walk-up? That location didn't deter my parents from making this move. Walking up and down four flights of stairs would become a mere inconvenience for them. Having his own private entrance, along with a bathroom inside the apartment, my father was ecstatic. He grew up on Henry Street on the Lower East Side of New York, where his family shared a bathroom in the hallway with four other families. I guess when a person grows up under those living conditions, one can understand how he might feel lucky.

However, my brother and I didn't feel so lucky when we had to haul groceries up four flights of stairs or when we had to endure many hot summers on the top floor of a building without any air conditioning.

My father had an interesting solution for our hot summer days. He installed a large fan in the window of our parlor to give us some relief. This fan was huge! The fan blade could have easily been used as a propeller on a Boeing Stratocruiser airplane. The only problem with this monstrosity, besides its deafening noise level, was that he always faced the fan outward. He was hoping that the hot air would escape the apartment, eventually cooling it down. He may have had the right theory about air movement, but with little to no breeze coming inside, the situation was futile. Additionally, the heat from the lower floors in the building would rise and accumulate on the top floor. A window air conditioner might have been a better option for us, but that was considered a luxury item back in the 1950s. As a result, we roasted in that apartment every summer and maybe lost some of our hearing, too.

My mother also had her own unique way of doing things. She refused to carry our laundry down four flights of stairs to the basement where the building's washing machine was located. I'm pretty sure the heavy lifting up and down the stairs wasn't the issue because my mother was as strong as an ox. Sharing the same washing machine with forty-five other tenants annoyed my germaphobe mother, who was fanatical about cleaning.

She proceeded to get on her hands and knees and use a washboard in our bathtub to clean our clothes. Can you imagine someone doing this laborious chore almost every day? She would then hang the wet clothes on a clothesline, four stories high, outside her bedroom window, reel them back in after they all had dried, then fold and put the clothes away. Oh, I forgot to mention, before putting everything in its place, she would take out her ironing board and iron every item. All the clothes, bedsheets, pillowcases, underwear, and even our handkerchiefs had to be ironed. Only our socks were spared that tedious process. What an outrageous routine. However, this was my mother's way of keeping her family in clean, neatly pressed, and germ-free clothes.

My mother and father, like many young immigrants, had to start working at an early age to help support their families. My mother was a seamstress who worked in a local sweatshop in Brooklyn. She would be paid pennies on the dollar for a completed garment. I remember she would be given a ticket for every finished clothing item. To receive a meager cash payment at the end of the workweek, she would tally all her tickets for submission to the shop foreman. She was not only poorly compensated but also denied fair working conditions.

Imagine many sewing machines all working simultaneously in tight quarters without the availability of air-conditioning or proper ventilation. The noise level and heat were probably brutal, but I never heard my mother complain about work. Maybe because she was a union member, she thought someday a pension would reward her for her hard work and dedication. And she was! If I remember correctly, when she retired, she received

$60 a month for all her years of service. That's about $180 these days. What a windfall.

My father was a truck driver who worked at the Fulton Fish Market in Lower Manhattan. He delivered fish in the Tri-State and surrounding areas. I remember him telling me the difficulty of securing a job during the Great Depression. He was ecstatic to land a job that he proudly boasted paid as much as a NYC police officer. He also experienced difficult working conditions. He was going in and out of a huge freezer every day. In all kinds of weather, he loaded and unloaded his truck with many bushels of fish. Each bushel weighed about 56 pounds. He left for work around 1 a.m. and returned home around midday. He drove his many routes in a truck that had a standard transmission, no power steering or power brakes. He didn't have the luxury of a navigation system or even a radio to learn about traffic conditions, but he, like my mother, never complained. He always came home with stories about his workday. Some were more interesting than others. Once he made a delivery to a golf country club and was inches away from Babe Ruth. He also mentioned that he had been good friends with heavyweight champ Floyd Patterson's father, who worked with him at the fish market.

One time in Lower Manhattan he witnessed a filming of a movie, starring American film actor George Raft. Many people around the set commented to my dad that he looked just like him. My father often repeated this story to me and anyone else who would listen, taking great pleasure in hearing that he looked like that actor. Personally, I think my dad was better looking than Mr. Raft. I guess you can say I'm partial. Maybe because I've been told that I look like my father.

Another perk that came along with his job were the many meals and other items he would receive during the course of his workday. He would sometimes get a sit-down lunch in the back of a restaurant, bring home a fresh pie or cake, or get some product samples from large consumer companies. We were never in need of aspirin, toothpaste, or many other consumer goods. Of course, there were always fresh fish, lobsters, and shrimp in our house on Fridays and most holidays. My father was also a card-carrying union member. For his forty years of service, he collected a whopping $340 a month after retiring. That would be about $1,300 a month now. Today, my parents combined income might cover some basic necessities, but not much more. The good old days.

My brother, Vincent (who I will refer to as Vinny going forward because I've never called him Vincent in my life) was seven years old when I came into this world. At that time, he was probably in the second grade at St. Frances de Chantal elementary school. Even at that very young age, Vinny quickly established himself as the adult in the room.

He always exhibited good judgment and common sense, which, unfortunately, were needed quite often at our kitchen table. Vinny would go on to be the voice of reason and guiding light in my life. My brother and I were named after our grandfathers, Vincenzo and Gaetano. Vinny once shared with me that at age seven he asked our parents why they didn't give me a middle name. My parents explained to him that he was given a middle name because of the events that occurred right after his birth. Vinny's middle name was Victor because he was born on May 7, 1945, which happened to be the day before VE Day (Victory in Europe Day). He wouldn't have had a middle name either if he hadn't been born that day. This logic would lead to my not having a middle name. My parents thought that nothing of any real significance happened on my birthday, October 1.

After doing some research, I did discover a few things that may have qualified as significant historical events. On October 1, 1908, Henry Ford's Model T went on sale to the public for the first time. Also on October 1, 1949, Chairman Mao Zedong, the leader of the Chinese Communist Party, declared the establishment of the People's Republic of China in Beijing. Luckily, these events in history didn't qualify as possible middle naming events. If my parents had been true historians, I could have possibly been named Thomas T. Grippa or Thomas Mao Zedong Grippa. I am happy my parents didn't know the history of the Ford Motor Company or that Chairman Mao's declaration wasn't front page news in the *Brooklyn Daily Eagle.*

I am also grateful that my birth wasn't delayed until October 31, because Biagio and Maria might have named me Thomas Trick-or-Treat Grippa! I'm pretty sure that at age seven, Vinny would have dropped his appeal for a middle name for me if any of those names had been discussed at the kitchen table. I'm good with no middle name—really, I am. Having fewer details to write on forms and applications has been a blessing in disguise.

CHAPTER TWO

My Pets

Surprisingly, I was allowed to have pets in our little apartment. My first pet was Goldie, a goldfish that we won at a feast at St. Finbar Church. We brought her home in a tiny round fishbowl that eventually turned into a full-size aquarium. However, she didn't really quench my thirst for a real pet that I could hold and cuddle with.

My next pet was Cecil the turtle, who would try to meet that expectation. My parents bought Cecil at a local pet shop in our neighborhood. The shopkeeper said these little turtles were easy to take care of and didn't require a lot of maintenance. He sold us a little plastic enclosure that featured steps and a plastic palm tree. We filled it with some water and fed Cecil his turtle food every day. The plastic enclosure needed to be cleaned at least once a week because Cecil wasn't the neatest tenant. On those occasions, I would let Cecil wander around on our linoleum floor in the parlor. Cecil seemed to enjoy his newfound freedom and would run as fast as he could to escape my clutches. Unfortunately, Cecil didn't last too long; we returned to the pet shop to get his brother. Cecil number two would go on to have a very short life span also. At that point, my mother decided that there would be no Cecil number three in my future since we killed enough of their family.

My next "victim" was Skipper, a green parakeet my father won at another church bazaar. At least he wasn't confined as Goldie to her aquarium or Cecil in his plastic palm tree enclosure. I could let him out of his cage and play with him in our apartment, or so I thought. One day Skipper was riding on my tricycle handlebars and enjoying the scenery in my parlor. Suddenly, Skipper must have gotten dizzy from riding around in circles for hours. He decided to leave me for higher terrain. He landed atop a mirror in our parlor. Well certainly, I couldn't leave my little feathered friend up there all by his lonesome. I proceeded to get on a chair and snatch Skipper from the top of that mirror.

One minor problem occurred with that swift and stupid move. Skipper, holding on for dear life, decided he didn't want any more excursions on my tricycle. Insisting my cuddly friend accompany me for another joy ride, I pulled a reluctant Skipper off that mirror. To my horror, one of his toenails remained there. Did you know a parakeet can fly widely around an apartment missing a toenail, for what seemed like hours? I sure didn't, but the blood he left everywhere in sight, including my parents' bedroom proved me wrong. Okay, it sounds like a gruesome sight, but Skipper survived this ordeal with my mom's quick thinking and action. She stopped his bleeding by putting his foot in flour.

After that fun and exciting experience, my parents decided Skipper needed a new home.

Skipper was relocated to my great aunt's apartment on New Utrecht Avenue. Zia Alfia was a widow who lived alone and needed a friend and companion more than I did. Besides, Skipper had a much greater chance of surviving in his new surroundings. Just ask Cecil number one and two.

Zia Alfia was a lot older than I and her bike-riding days were well behind her. She would protect and care for our little feathered friend till his dying days. He would go on to live for many years with our dear, sweet aunt. Skipper was so happy to be in his new home with Zia Alfia that he even took up a second language. He learned to speak Italian so he could converse with our aunt. And that, my friend, is not a joke. That parakeet had a better command of the Sicilian dialect than I ever had. He may have become bilingual at Zia Alfia's apartment, but just remember who taught Skipper how to ride on a bike.

After a few years without any pets, I focused my attention on getting a dog. Our neighbor in the apartment across the hall had a miniature pinscher named Penny. From ages four to seven, I had regular playdates with Penny. She was so much fun. Fetching, running around, and doing tricks were pretty much the extent of our playing time together. Thank goodness Penny couldn't fly, or my mom might have been called into action again. Anyway, my experience with Penny made me want my own dog. My parents wouldn't hear it. Our apartment was too small for a dog, they said.

I argued that Penny lived next door in an apartment just like ours. This discussion went on for several years until I was about eleven. At last, my parents relented and purchased a puppy for me. I'm pretty sure my nagging and constant torturing of them had absolutely nothing to do with their sudden change of heart. In fact, I'm willing to bet my Catholic school experience had a lot to do with it. More on that later.

After a day of whining and crying from seeing my furry friend in a pet store window on 86th Street in Bensonhurst, the time for dog ownership had finally come. My brother was given the assignment of taking me back to the pet store after dinner to pick up our new dog. Daisy was a purebred black-and-white toy fox terrier. For the mere sum of $35 (about $367 today), my new companion was relocating to Boro Park to be with her new family. Little did we know, Daisy must have been reincarnated from someone with Italian DNA.

My parents, whose only experience of taking care of four legged creatures was Cecil's one and two, decided to feed Daisy Italian meals instead of dog food; I guess because the turtle food hadn't worked out so well for her reptile predecessors. She would eat everything my mother had prepared for us. To further prove her Italian heritage, she would only eat her food if it had grated Parmesan cheese on it. Even a breakfast meal of scrambled eggs had to have some Italian cheese sprinkled on it.

My mother would sometimes test her and leave the cheese out of her food. That dog would sniff around and then stare at her dish all day until that Parmesan came out of the fridge.

Daisy was never going to grow into a large dog, which was one of the prerequisites of my negotiated deal with my parents. Also, I had to promise to take care of Daisy. I agreed, but, as you may have guessed, how many eleven-year-olds hold up that end of the bargain? I was no different. However, I did ensure that Daisy would get her daily exercise outside. Almost every evening after supper, my dad and I would take Daisy on our roof. I would chase her around and throw clothespins for her to fetch. One evening, I tossed a clothespin off the four-story building. My dog, Daisy, bolted after it. Instead of leaping over the short brick ledge, she stopped abruptly and peered through a space between the bricks to see where the clothespin had fallen. Had Daisy's brakes failed, I'd likely still be in therapy.

That dog truly lived a charmed life. I'll recount another of Daisy's close calls in chapter 17, when we moved to Gravesend, Brooklyn.

CHAPTER THREE
Apartment Life

Four people living in a three-room apartment had its disadvantages. We were always on top of one another. My mom pretty much stayed in the kitchen all day preparing meals or chatting with family and friends on our only telephone in the apartment. My dad came home from work in the early afternoon and would sit in our parlor reading his newspaper. My brother could be found in my parents' bedroom, doing his homework, playing with his microscope, or listening to his records on the Victrola. A Victrola was a phonograph that was made by the RCA Victor Company. My grandkids can look up the definition of both phonographs and records at their leisure. That pretty much left me in the parlor playing with my toys or watching our small Zenith black-and-white television, which, at that time, offered a limited selection of children's programming.

Sleeping arrangements became a challenge in our small apartment. Not having our own bedroom, my brother and I had to sleep in the parlor on a Castro Convertible. If you have never heard of this product, a Castro Convertible was a couch that folded open into a bed. Not sure if they bought that brand because its inventor, Bernard Castro, was of Sicilian origin or because the Castro Convertibles were the only game in town.

My guess is the latter. Mr. Castro invented a great product for families who didn't have a second bedroom. I wish he had made that darn mattress just a little thicker. My brother and I still have the battle scars from that early childhood sleeping experience.

Our cramped living space affected the number of toys and games we could keep and offered no room for friends to visit. Only on Halloween did I feel as if I had a distinct advantage over my friends, who had their own houses. Living in an apartment building with forty-five households, I didn't have to walk very far or deal with the outside elements to do my trick-or-treating. I felt so fortunate to bring home all those decaying apples with pennies lodged in them. Yum! I also received unwrapped and loose goodies like candy corn, M&M's, bubble gum, lollipops, and homemade cookies. I was allowed to keep only the wrapped items and the pennies of course. It still felt like a treasure trove to this little kid. Once I got older, I was able to venture onto the city streets to solicit treats from my friends' homes also. Their parents were very generous with their treats, especially to the friendly faces they recognized. There were no decaying apples with pennies in them being distributed on 58th Street.

Since the parlor was my playground during the day, I had to come up with things to do to keep myself occupied. One day before my dad got home from work, I decided to test my archery skills with a new bow-and-arrow set my parents had gotten me.

The set came with a target, a bow and arrows, which had rubber suction cups on the tips. I thought a good idea would be to place the target in front of my parents' glass bookcase, which housed our new *Encyclopedia Britannica*. Well, this four-year-old didn't have the steadiest hands as he pulled back on that bow. I hit the bookcase glass instead of the target's bull's-eye and shattered the glass into a million pieces. Thinking I had just put my head through the glass bookcase, my mother came running into the parlor. She assumed I had been taking another spin on my tricycle. Relieved that I was okay, she cleaned up the mess and said, "Your father isn't going to be very happy about this." And he sure wasn't.

After calming down, he measured the opening and remaining sliding glass door and went to the store to order a replacement. He picked up our new glass door a few weeks later and placed it into the bookcase. Dad's measurement could have been a tad off or maybe the glass maker needed a new pair of glasses himself. Whatever the reason, it was virtually impossible to slide the new glass door from one side to the other. When my brother had to use the encyclopedias and needed a volume on the "wrong side" of the bookcase, he would have to remove all the volumes from the "good side" to get to it. Like my father, Vinny wasn't too pleased with my archery skills, especially after doing some research for a homework assignment. Unfortunately, there was no Google in 1956.

When I wasn't wreaking havoc in the parlor with my pets, tricycle, or bow and arrow, I spent most of my mornings in my parents' bedroom. Vinny spent the late afternoons there doing his homework or listening to his records. This became our shared recreation room when my parents were at work. During the week, Zia Alfia, who spoke very little English, took care of me. Other than watching television or playing with my toys, there wasn't much to keep me occupied during the day.

When Vinny got home from school, he would be spinning his 45s on our Victrola. He had a huge rock-and-roll record collection. He purchased many of his own records, and his collection was supplemented by family members on special occasions. I could hear the records he was playing every day from our parlor. I was enjoying the music from a distance even at the early ages of five and six. When my parents' bedroom became available, Zia Alfia would let me play my brother's records to my heart's content. That poor lady heard the same few records being played day after day, sometimes for hours at a time. This six-year-old DJ was spinning records like Murray the K and Cousin Brucie. I had several favorites, including "Susie Darlin'" by Robin Luke,

"You're So Fine" by The Falcons, and "Rebel Rouser" by Duane Eddy. This early appreciation for rock-and-roll music turned me into an old soul.

As I was growing up, most of my friends were into sixties' and seventies' music. Thanks to my older brother, I was stuck in the fifties—and I enjoyed every minute of it. These many years later, I'm finally in my element because I look like everyone else at the oldies shows that Vinny and I attend with our wives. I can easily be mistaken as Vinny's older brother because of my height advantage and my hair-follicle deficiencies. All's good—since I wouldn't want to be enjoying those oldies but goodies with anyone else!

CHAPTER FOUR

The Block

A street where kids always played or gravitated to in Brooklyn was called "The Block." Our neighborhood block in Boro Park was 58th Street between 14th and 15th Avenue. That block was my world, my universe, until I reached the age of eleven. My best friend, Tommy, lived right in the middle of the block in a two-family home. Across the street were our other friends Paul, Johnny, Elena, and Louise.

Tommy lived downstairs with his parents; his older brother, Jamie; and his younger sisters, Lizzie and Marian. His aunt, uncle, and their two boys, Johnny and Bobby, lived on the second floor. Johnny and Bobby, coincidentally, were good friends with my brother, Vinny.

I first met Tommy in our grammar school, St. Frances de Chantal, located on 13th Avenue. Kismet must have brought this group of friends together. (Growing up in Boro Park, Brooklyn, you pick up some Yiddishisms along the way. Get used to it, as I often use these words in this book.) Yes, kismet was responsible for my having the same circle of friends on 58th Street as my brother. My parents didn't have to worry about their little boy on the streets of Brooklyn, since I was in a known, safe place, chaperoned by my older brother. My dad would go up on the roof, whistle, and we would suddenly appear in his sights.

By the way, that whistle came like clockwork, at 6 p.m. every day, to alert us that dinner was on the table. I spent almost every waking moment on that block, mostly around Tommy's house.

We played basketball and Ping-Pong in his backyard, stoopball on his front steps, and when I was older, stickball on 58th Street.

Stoopball is loosely based on the game of baseball. The batter threw a rubber ball, usually a Spalding (called a *Spaldeen* in Brooklyn) or Pensie Pinkie, against the stoop, which are steps in front of a home. A Spaldeen was a light pink-colored rubber ball that was hard and highly inflated, for a higher bounce. A Pensie Pinkie was a darker pink rubber ball, which was a little less inflated and softer to the touch. It was a little more forgiving than a Spaldeen.

The object of the game was to land the ball behind the fielder. The result would be a single, double, triple, or home run based on the number of times the ball bounced before one got to it. If a player caught it in the air or the ball traveled less than to the designated spot, the result was an out. At least that was how we played stoopball on 58th Street.

Stickball was another variation of a baseball game where we used a broom handle as a bat. One could have also purchased a stickball bat at the local mom-and-pop grocery store. That stick was a little thicker than a broom handle and would also have black tape around the bottom where one gripped it. Again, using a Spaldeen or Pensie Pinkie, stickball could be played in several ways on a street.

A player could self-pitch by throwing the ball into the air, letting it bounce once or twice, and then swinging his stickball bat. Or one could play with a pitcher who could manipulate the ball to do tricks, making it bounce left, right, or even forward. Regardless of how the game was played, a large playing field was required to truly enjoy the game. Fifty-eighth Street between 14th and 15th Avenue, both with parked cars and oncoming traffic, was our version of Ebbets Field. First and third base were usually car parts like a door handle or fender. Second base was usually a sewer cover in the middle of the street, just beyond first and third. If a ball traveled three sewers, it was usually a home run. All other hits were determined on that narrow street by the ball placement, the base runner's speed, and the defense.

Games were usually halted when the ball would travel to a sewer grate and drop into the city's sewage system. Countless Spaldeen and Pensie Pinky balls found their final resting place in the sewers of Brooklyn.

Tommy's stoop also served as our grandstand to watch our older siblings, cousins, and their friends play stickball. They were much more proficient at the game than we were. And when no game was being played, that stoop became our central meeting place to discuss world events. Most times those discussions revolved around our favorite sports teams, that night's TV schedule, or what we were having for dinner.

Speaking of dinner, one of my fondest memories was being at Tommy's house while his mom was making her tomato sauce. And, yes, it's *sauce*, not *gravy*! Some Italians call tomato sauce gravy. Gravy goes on meatloaf or mashed potatoes, not pasta! There are no "tomato gravy cans" on supermarket shelves. As Tommy's mom's sauce simmered on her stovetop, she would invite the kids to sample it. After having sliced a fresh Italian bread, she would dip it into her sauce and hand us our treat. That experience was way better than any trip to the candy store. That slice of Italian bread was a special treat for all Tommy's friends. She was a wonderful lady.

On the corner of 58th Street and 14th Avenue was Henry's Grocery Store. Henry and his wife, Regina, primarily operated that grocery store with some assistance from Regina's mother. Henry and Regina were pleasant people, but her mom had a little edge to herself. She had a mean streak and had no tolerance for little squirts like us. She was strictly business, no small talk. When she did speak, she would usually tell us to buy something or get out of the store.

Their most memorable employee at the store was Murray, whose primary responsibility was to deliver groceries. Murray was a large, kind, gentle man in his thirties or forties who was developmentally challenged. Murray would push a large wooden cart filled with bagged groceries and personal items throughout our neighborhood. He would be singing inaudible sounds to himself as he pushed his wagon through the streets. We always loved our verbal exchanges when Murray came down our block.

Whoever spotted Murray first would give out a loud shout, "Hey, Murrayyyyyyyy!"

He would respond in kind with a loud "Heyyyyyyyy!" Kinda like Fat Albert of Bill Cosby fame.

Our exchanges may sound dopey, but that silly banter is forever embedded in my brain. Who knew all these years later that Murray would become the precursor to Amazon and Instacart. The man was a genius! We all loved him.

One day Murray failed to show up for work. His pushcart was filled with groceries ready to be delivered. My then ten-year-old brother happened to be shopping for candy at the grocery store when Henry approached him with an interesting proposition. He said, "Grippa"— Henry knew us kids by our last names only—"Murray is not here; how would you like to make his deliveries today? I'll give you fifteen cents a delivery plus tips."

My brother, always the entrepreneur, emphatically said, "Sure."

Henry then labeled every grocery bag in Murray's cart and sent Vinny off to make the deliveries. Picture this little ten-year-old kid heading down the street and pushing a large cart filled with groceries. People in the neighborhood took notice since Vinny wasn't singing to himself and he wasn't a large six-foot-one adult. One such neighbor recognized Vinny and knocked on our door to inform my mother of Vinny's new employment.

My mother couldn't believe her ears. She said, "My son is pushing Murray's cart in the neighborhood?"

Why was this so upsetting to my mother, you ask? She, like most Italian mothers, placed great importance on maintaining a good public image. She was always concerned about how we were perceived by the public. She thought people would see her oldest son as having a disability similar to Murray's. When my brother got home from his hard day at work, my mother was waiting for him at the front door. She said, "You are never to make any deliveries for Henry's grocery store again."

Now my brother couldn't believe his ears. "Mom, what are you talking about? I made over three dollars today. It was easy money. I'm the only ten-year-old on the block with a part-time job."

"I don't care how much money you made. You are never to push Murray's cart in the streets again. You understand!"

My brother reluctantly agreed and retreated to my parents' bedroom to do his homework. When my father got home, my mother explained what had happened earlier that day. My father took my brother's side and said there had been absolutely nothing wrong with him having made grocery deliveries in the neighborhood. Murray's unfortunate condition was not contagious.

At that point, my mother must have realized how silly she had sounded. So, after that day, my brother became Murray's official pinch hitter whenever Henry needed him to step up to the plate. He would fill in from time to time and be the only ten-year-old in our neighborhood with some money in his pockets. Vinny spread his wealth by treating his friends to ice cream and candy on many occasions. His work ethic became common knowledge in the neighborhood. He would eventually get a permanent part-time job delivering drycleaning for Bunny's Dry Cleaners. Vinny would now use his bike for deliveries instead of a pushcart.

Henry was a hardworking, decent guy. He took orders from our parents in person or over the phone and packaged everything for delivery by our dear friend Murray. Seemingly, Henry worked 24/7. He was always visible at his corner store.

One day my father, mother and I were returning home from shopping. I must have been three or four. My dad parked his car right across the street from Henry's Grocery Store. When I got out of the car, for some stupid reason, I suddenly ran to the fire alarm box on the corner, reached up, and pulled the handle. Please don't ask me what I was thinking at the time; three- and four-year-olds don't always think. The fire alarm box emitted a loud sounding alarm. With both hands positioned above his head, my father screamed, "What did you just do?"

I thought that was a rhetorical question, but I answered it anyway. "I pulled the fire alarm, Dad!"

He said, "Quick, quick, we need to run upstairs before the fire engines get here."

Off we went, under the watchful eye of Henry the Grocer. Minutes later, with what seemed like a battalion of fire trucks, our block was surrounded. I couldn't tell you how many showed up since I was neatly positioned under my parents' bed. I did, however, hear my parents' conversation very clearly from my position. They were imagining whether Henry would be turning me into the coppers. To our surprise, no policeman came knocking on our door that afternoon to arrest me. I eventually came out from under the bed because dinner was on the table. In the days and weeks following, Henry never said a word to my parents or me about the incident he had witnessed. As I said, Henry was a decent guy.

One lasting memory of the block was my unofficial designation of being the Shabbos goy. A Shabbos goy is a non-Jew who performs such tasks as turning the lights and gas on and off for religious Jews on the Sabbath. When I asked my dad if entering peoples' homes would be acceptable, he said yes. He went on to say that when he had been a young boy growing up on the Lower East Side, he did the exact same thing for people. He was delighted that I was willing to provide this service, without any prior knowledge of his similar childhood experience.

Nice to know that on my block, I was a chip off the old block.

For the record, I still hold the title of Shabbos goy in my house as I continue to turn off lights for my Jewish wife, Tina. Though my actions are more pragmatic than religious now, I often wonder if she is a stockholder in our electricity provider. If we were back in Brooklyn, I'd ask, like lots of parents did when someone left the lights on (usually us kids), "Do you own stock in Con Edison?"

CHAPTER FIVE

The Neighborhood

As in most neighborhoods in Brooklyn, there were specific places of business and houses of worship that were common to us all. We had our candy store, luncheonette, pizza place, bakery, movie theater, bowling alley, and neighborhood church or synagogue. You get the point. Boro Park was no different. We had our favorites, but only a few of these places stood out in my mind as I was writing this book.

The first was Savarese Italian Pastry Shoppe on 59th Street and New Utrecht Avenue. It's still there today, but I'm unsure if it's under the same family ownership as it was in the fifties and sixties. My parents went there for pastries, cakes, cannoli, and cookies. I have no recollection of how these things tasted, but I'm pretty sure they were all very good. I do have a vivid memory of their Italian ices, specifically their lemon ice. It was like a little scoop of heaven in that little white crushable cup. I became a frequent visitor to Savarese, only two short blocks from our apartment building, for their lemon ice. I blame my current waistline and gross tonnage entirely on them.

I seem to recall hearing Groucho Marx ask a female contestant on his game show *You Bet Your Life*, "What's your gross tonnage?" referring to her weight. Groucho would surely not get away with that remark today, but it was pretty funny to me then.

My next sweet tooth shop in Boro Park was Lazareth's luncheonette, also on New Utrecht Avenue. Lazareth's offered breakfast, lunch, and soda fountain service to its patrons. Going and coming from St. Frances de Chantal, we walked by that luncheonette every school day. My friends and I went there on our way home from school. Sometimes I wished Lazareth's had a real bar, instead of a soda fountain counter, so I could have an adult beverage after a day with those nuns. (I must admit that this thought just popped into my head.) Instead of ordering a stiff one, I calmed down at the soda counter with my daily Lime Rickey, which consisted of lime juice, club soda, and sugar. Most kids had egg creams at that counter, but I couldn't. I thought the soda jerk put a raw egg in egg creams, and I wanted no part of that until I found out its actual ingredients were seltzer water, chocolate syrup (usually Fox's U-Bet), and milk. You may ask where I got the notion that raw eggs were ingredients in egg creams? Well, my mom, concerned with my nutritional health, always slipped a raw egg into my egg creams and milkshakes at home. I thought for sure she told the owners of Lazareth's to do the same thing. Stupid me, I missed out on some really good stuff at Lazareth's in those early years. Thanks, Mom.

As for most kids growing up in Brooklyn, one of our favorite pastimes was bowling. In Boro Park, there were two bowling alleys that I often enjoyed. One was Maple Lanes, located off 16th Avenue and 60th Street. This forty-eight-lane masterpiece was built in 1960. It was one of the largest bowling alleys in all of Brooklyn. Maple Lanes was a great place to go to have fun with friends. Some of us had serious aspirations of becoming the next PBA National Champion like Don Carter or Dick Weber.

Since that goal was never going to be a reality in my lifetime because I was a horrible bowler, I preferred trying my hand at duckpin bowling, which was bowling on a much smaller scale. Duckpin bowling balls were smaller in diameter and weight. Without finger holes, the balls would be thrown underhanded, by holding the ball in the palm of your hand. The duckpins were slightly thinner and carried less weight than their regular counterparts. Because of these differences from regular bowling, achieving a strike was more difficult. Therefore, duckpin bowlers were allowed three rolls per frame instead of two. Strikes still could be achieved with one's first throw and spares with two throws.

Olympia Lanes was a duckpin bowling alley located on a second floor of a building along New Utrecht Avenue near 51st Street in Boro Park. Pin boys arranged the duckpins, identical to regular bowling pins, into a triangle. They also were responsible for returning the ball to the bowler. Automation was scarce in that duckpin bowling center. Although this game was more fun for a skinny little kid, I could not master this form of bowling either.

I eventually gave up the sport until we relocated to the Gravesend section of Brooklyn where my bowling spirit got rekindled with league play at Shell Lanes. I never won a trophy or broke 200, but I shared many good times there with my friends.

Brooklyn is responsible for two PBA Hall of Famers, Mark Roth, who attained thirty-four PBA Tour titles in his career, and Johnny Petraglia, who won fourteen PBA Tour titles and eight PBA Senior titles. He also rolled a perfect 300 game at age forty-seven.

We visited two movie theaters in Boro Park when I was a kid. The Boro Park and the Loew's 46th Street theaters. The movie theater I preferred was the larger Loew's 46th Street Theater on New Utrecht Avenue between 46th and 45th streets. It was a majestic theater built in 1927. To this little kid, this was Boro Park's answer to the Radio City Musical Hall. We loved seeing movies in such a large, beautiful venue. One day in 1963, my mother and aunt took my cousins and me to see *The Nutty Professor* starring Jerry Lewis. In addition to viewing this newly released movie, we were looking forward to seeing Jerry Lewis, who would be making a personal appearance that day. Every kid was enamored with Jerry Lewis at that time, and we were no different. I remember being so excited to see him in person, on stage, in Boro Park of all places.

Jerry did make an appearance. He walked onto the stage, said a few words, and then he quickly left the building. His hit-and-run appearance surprised me. I expected him to tell us some jokes, take a few pratfalls, shoot seltzer water into the audience, or start a pie-throwing fight, but none of that happened. I would have even been thrilled if he had just run down the aisle near me before jumping onto the stage. His personal appearance was a very anticlimactic event. However, *The Nutty Professor* did turn out to be a pretty good movie to this eleven-year-old critic.

Another memory I have is of my parents taking us shopping for shoes at the Buster Brown Shoe store on 13th Avenue. For some unknown reason, they were convinced that Buster Brown shoes were of a higher quality than that of other brands available at that time. One distinct advantage was that we would receive a Buster Brown comic book with every purchase. On one visit to the store our Buster Brown comic book featured a drawing contest where kids could win prizes for coloring in a picture. First prize was a brand-new bicycle. Second prize was a radio. My coloring skills weren't fully developed at that point in my life; I didn't even attempt it. My older brother, Vinny, wanted to give it his best shot in this competition. He colored in the picture and asked our dad to mail it to the "Buster Brown" TV show. Smilin' Ed McConnell hosted this weekly TV show, which was actually called *Smilin' Ed McConnell and His Buster Brown Gang*. Winners were going to be announced and featured on the show later that month. When my father saw my brothers' picture, he asked for my comic book. My dad went to printing school, and he had artistic ability way beyond that of the children in his household. He took out his artist coloring pencils and proceeded to do his thing.

He was always drawing pictures he would see in *LIFE* magazine. Two of his best drawings were of Pope Pius XII and Pope John XXIII, which he proudly displayed in our *Encyclopedia Britannica* bookcase. I'm pretty sure I actually hit one of them, right between the eyes, with my bow and arrow. When my dad finished his coloring project, he told Vinny that he was going to enter his drawing into the contest instead of my brother's, but he would put Vinny's name on the drawing. Dad felt his own drawing had a greater chance of winning than Vinny's. I guess he felt coloring within the lines was an important factor in determining the eventual winner. Thinking neither of them had a legitimate shot of winning this contest anyway, my brother went along with his suggestion.

A few weeks later, my brother received a letter from the "Buster Brown" TV show. They congratulated Vinny for having finished in second place in the drawing contest. He was the winner of a Motorola radio. All he had to do was appear on the TV show in a few weeks to get his prize. My brother told my parents that he had no intention of going on that TV program to claim his prize. He thought that the producers of the show, to ensure he was the actual artist, would ask him to replicate what my father had done. The chances of this happening were slim, but Vinny wasn't taking any chances. My parents begged him to change his mind because they wanted him to have that radio. Vinny was adamant about not embarrassing himself on national television and this stalemate went on for over a week. My parents finally gave up and reluctantly decided to forgo the second-place prize.

Unfortunately, Ed McConnell suddenly died of a heart attack the following week. The show wouldn't resume production until the following year with Andy Devine as its new host. Vinny received his new Motorola radio in the mail a few weeks later. My parents never expected to see their child so cheerful over the demise of a TV personality.

The Church of St. Rosalia and St. Frances de Chantal were two churches in Boro Park that I visited frequently. St. Rosalia, where my mother and father got married, was located on 63rd Street and 14th Avenue in Boro Park. St. Frances de Chantal was my family's new parish because it had a parochial school that my brother and I would eventually attend. I was at St. Rosalia every weekday morning for early mass. My mother's aunt, Zia Alfia, belonged to that parish. In addition to being Skipper's new mommy, she also was responsible for my care until I reached school age. With both my parents working, Zia Alfia brought me along on her daily pilgrimage to that church. Daily Mass could be a little monotonous for a fidgety five-year-old. One day I resisted going to church with Zia. She said, "Fine" probably in Italian since she spoke very little English. She proceeded to make me understand that I should sit on the top step near the church front entrance and wait for her return. Not exactly a good idea, even in 1957. I sat there that day waiting for mass to be over when a very friendly-looking dog approached me.

Well, you know how much I love animals, so I tried to pet this little pooch. He wasn't as friendly as I had thought. He unexpectedly took a bite out of my hand and ran away. Bleeding now, I decided the time had come for me to find some religion. I went into church for redemption and a handkerchief from Zia. She saw me bleeding and rushed me home to my apartment. While cleaning me up and bandaging me, she was speaking Sicilian at a frantic pace. I assume the translation was something like, *How could I be so stupid, as to leave a five-year-old alone, outside of a church?* Or, *My niece is going to kill me, for being so stupid as to leave a five-year-old alone, outside of a church?* Or maybe she was just muttering some new words for Skipper to learn later that day. Anyway, we both awaited my father's arrival from work that afternoon. When my dad got home, Zia explained what had happened to me.

My father in his always calming demeanor shouted, "We have to go find that dog and make sure he doesn't have rabies!"

"What is rabies, Dad?" I asked.

"Never mind, but we have to find that dog or you're getting injections in your stomach!"

"Yipes! Shots in my stomach! Heck no! Let's go, Pop! I'll ride shotgun in the car!"

We proceeded to drive around St. Rosalia's church in pursuit of that very bad dog.

Luckily, after a few spins around the block, lo and behold, we saw Sparky locked in a front gate of a home. My dad went to the front door to speak to the owner and found out Sparky was current with all his vaccines. I was saved from those darn rabies shots in my stomach.

Here's the moral of this story: Don't pet stray animals and go to church with your *famiglia*.

CHAPTER SIX

My Extended Famiglia

My parents, Vinny, and I visited with my aunts and uncles regularly. We would rotate weekends seeing Aunt Millie and Uncle Bennie, first in their apartment in Brooklyn, then in their new home on Long Island. On alternate weekends, we would visit Aunt Dolly and Uncle Benny, in their Lower Manhattan apartment, then in their new home in New Jersey. In between, we would visit Aunt Lucy and Uncle Joe in their Brooklyn apartment. When we weren't visiting these relatives, they were visiting us. If you haven't noticed, Italians do a lot of visiting.

Aunt Lucia, known as Aunt Lucy, was my mother's older sister. She had two sons (Francesco and Gaetano) and two daughters (Antonina and Maria). Aunt Carmella, whom we called Aunt Millie, was my mom's younger sister. She had two sons (Albert and Thomas) and a daughter (Annette). Aunt Dolly, whose given name was Josephine, had four boys (Joseph, Fredrick, Anthony, and Robert). As you can see, there were plenty of cousins to visit at every family gathering.

Uncle Benny from New Jersey had the same name as my father Biagio. Both were named after their paternal grandfather. In reality, he was my father's first cousin, but my dad always referred to him as his older brother because they had grown up in the same household as siblings. This arranged family dynamic occurred when my father's father, Vincenzo, died in battle during World War I. With no visible means of support in Sicily, his wife, Carmella, came to America with her six-year-old child (my dad) to marry her brother-in-law, Giuseppe. He too, was a widower in need of a companion to take care of his eight-year-old son (Uncle Benny). Pairing up family members who were in dire situations was quite common in those days. This arranged marriage resulted in two cousins with the same name becoming brothers. Just wanted to point that out, as it wasn't a similar situation to Heavyweight Champion George Foreman, who named all five of his sons George. He once said, "I named all my sons George Edward Foreman so they would always have something in common." Having the same grandparents and experiencing the loss of a parent would be something the two Biagios would always have in common.

    My grandmother Carmella and great-uncle Giuseppe were married for twelve years when she suddenly passed from an unknown illness. He would later go on to marry his third wife Alfia, who happened to be my mother's aunt. The same aunt eventually became our parakeet Skipper's new mommy. I told you, the families were very close. She would play a prominent role in my early childhood years. Zia Alfia was like a grandmother to me.

    My maternal grandparents still considered Sicily their permanent home when I was young. Zia Alfia would babysit and take care of me so my mom could return to work.

    Do you need a family tree chart or baseball scorecard at this point in the story to follow all the individual and player movement? Don't feel bad; I have shared this family history with my wife, kids, and grandkids many times, and they still don't get it. We had two brothers with the same name. My dad's aunt was married to my mother's uncle. My mom's aunt was my father's stepmother. Skipper had two mommies. The mid-twentieth century comedy team Bud Abbott and Lou Costello's "Who's on First?" routine would be easier to decipher.

    Being cooped up in that apartment every day, we looked

forward to visiting our relatives in the suburbs. Heck, we even looked forward to going to their apartments in Brooklyn, too. Seeing my relatives, eating good food, playing games, and just enjoying one another's company was always special. The most fun I had was on Long Island with my cousins, who were closer in age to me. They had an above-ground swimming pool in their backyard and an open field across the street where we could shoot BB guns, simulate war games, or play catch. We also played with toy dinosaurs, built underground tunnels, and shot off water rockets in that field. When Uncle Bennie got his first boat, we would go fishing and crabbing in the Great South Bay. All these things were completely foreign to a kid from Brooklyn. We couldn't replicate these activities in our schoolyard.

It was truly an outdoor adventure for me. Even their ice cream man was different. We had the Good Humor Man in Brooklyn. They had a guy with a Bungalow Bar truck. The kids would say, "Bungalow Bar tastes like tar, the more you eat it, the sicker you are." For the record, it never made me sick.

Going to New Jersey was fun, too. My cousin Robert would let me play on his drums, and Anthony would take us to get "A'beetsa" from the local pizzeria. It was always great whether it was purchased on Mott Street or in Rutherford, New Jersey. I always loved hearing my father and uncle speaking with such great passion to one another. Sometimes they sounded like two volcanoes erupting. When I would ask my mother why they yelled at each other every time they got together, she would reply, "They're not yelling at one another; they're Italian; that's how they speak."

Things were a little calmer at Aunt Lucy's home. Maybe because everyone primarily spoke Sicilian there. Aunt Lucy's family were the last close relatives to immigrate to our country. Some of my older cousins weren't very happy about leaving Sicily and their friends behind. However, my aunt and uncle felt it was the right time for this life-changing move to America. There were many more job opportunities in this country, and most of our family was now residing in Brooklyn.

When my aunt and uncle finally decided to come to America, they moved in with our Zia Alfia temporarily until they could find employment and permanent housing. Zia had a very large apartment that could accommodate her six new family members. The biggest adjustment they had to make was in dealing with the "EL" (elevated train line), which was adjacent to the apartment.

They had come from a quiet little farm in Sicily. They would now be dealing with a rumbling train that would pass by their windows every fifteen to twenty minutes. The sound was so intense that it would reverberate throughout the apartment and shake the floors with each passing train. This took some getting used to. It would be just over a year before they found their own place to live. When we visited my aunt and uncle, only their children would speak English. I remember thinking, *Why doesn't everyone speak English here?* They had been in the country for a while, but Sicilian was the preferred language at our family gatherings. It bothered me since I was always wondering what they were talking and laughing about. I did come to understand the Sicilian language as the years passed, but it was always a struggle for me. Today, I wish I could go back in time and hear it all over again, as it was a beautiful language spoken by beautiful people. I didn't really appreciate it as much as I should have.

Now when I long to hear some Sicilian talk, I have to watch a rerun of *The Godfather,* especially the scene where Michael dines with Sollozzo and McCluskey before filling them full of lead. I know that seems silly, but Sollozzo and Michael spoke the exact same Sicilian dialect I had heard in our homes, and, no, we never discussed the family business at the dining room table. We had no family business. We did, however, play Italian card games like Sette e mezzo ("seven and a half") and Catarina at that table. Uncle Joe had two mandolins at his apartment. He would always let me play one of them when we visited. His was a beautiful-sounding instrument that I butchered as a youngster. We also ate the greatest homemade pizza at that dining room table. Aunt Lucy could whip up enough pizza pies in her small oven to feed an army. Every ingredient was natural and made from scratch. I have tried to replicate that recipe many times, but nothing has ever come close to Aunt Lucy's "A'beetsa."

I loved everyone in my extended family, but I had a real soft spot in my heart for Aunt Millie. She was like my second mother. When I was around four or five, my mother had to go into the hospital for a hysterectomy. My father and brother took me to Long Island for a surprise two-week vacation. Not one word was uttered about my vacation plans the entire drive there. I guess my parents thought keeping me in the dark and suddenly taking off would be a great idea.

After eating lunch, my father and brother did their Houdini act and disappeared. *Poof,* they were gone as my Aunt Millie distracted me. As you can imagine, their disappearance did not go well. I cried and cried that my family had abandoned me. Aunt Millie consoled me and explained that my situation was temporary until my mother got better. She assured me they were coming back to get me in two weeks and that I would soon be returning to the friendly confines of Brooklyn.

During that extended stay my aunt and I became very close. That bond we developed would remain intact for the rest of our lives. Spending so much time with my aunt and uncle on Long Island, I also grew closer to Uncle Bennie. As previously mentioned, he enjoyed taking me fishing and crabbing on his boat. He also became my hero when my cousin Albert accidentally broke my new toy rifle. This rifle was very special to me as it was a replica of the rifle used on the TV show *The Rifleman,* starring Chuck Connors. I couldn't wait to show the rifle to my cousins. Unfortunately, the plastic butt of the rifle cracked into a million pieces. I was totally devastated. When my uncle got home from work, he took the rifle from me and said, "Don't worry, this will be as good as new the next time you come to visit us."

As I left to go back to Brooklyn, I was thinking to myself, *How the heck is he going to glue Humpty Dumpty back together again?* When I returned in a few weeks, I was expecting to see a partially glued, duct-taped butt on the end of my Rifleman's gun. Instead, to my surprise, my uncle handed me the rifle with a new buttstock made of wood.

He had whittled a piece of pine into the exact shape of the plastic piece that had broken. He sanded, stained, and polyurethaned it to make it look like a real rifle. His workmanship and creativity were off the charts! I actually had a better, more realistic-looking rifle than the one that had come off the store shelf. Only Uncle Bennie would have taken the time and effort to make this little kid feel so special. He showed his affection in many other ways, too. When we went fishing, he would take me out to lunch at a waterfront restaurant. He let me order any sandwich I wanted. He treated me as one of his buddies. When I needed to choose a sponsor for my confirmation, he became the easy choice. I'll never forget how he was brought to tears when I asked him and again at the church ceremony. He was a special guy.

One last thing about my extended family comes to mind: Our cousins are really our first forever friends. We share an ancestry and common bond that cannot be broken. Even as we age and might not see each other as frequently as we had as children, that closeness and love all come back to us the minute we lay eyes on one another.

CHAPTER SEVEN

Bye-Bye, Dodgers! Hello, Mets!

In 1955 the Dodgers were coming off their World Series win over the hated Yankees. It was their first World Series win over their cross-town rivals. The Brooklyn Dodger fans were euphoric with the team's unexpected win. Gil Hodges had a historical record-breaking performance in game seven. He drove in the only two runs the Dodgers would score in a seventh and deciding World Series game.

Gil Hodges was Vinny's favorite player. My dad had heard on the radio that Gil Hodges and other Dodger players would be making a personal appearance and signing autographs at a neighborhood appliance store. Back in the fifties, baseball players were not compensated as they are today. In the offseason, they would take odd jobs and make personal appearances to supplement their income. My dad asked Vinny if he wanted to go to the store that day to see his Dodger heroes. My ten-year-old brother didn't hesitate when he responded that he was totally onboard with my father's plan for the day. Unfortunately, when they got to the store, they witnessed a line of kids that extended way beyond the entrance of the appliance store. They asked people waiting in line which Dodger players were inside the store. They discovered that only two Dodgers were at this event.

That long line leading out of the store was for a chance to meet Dodgers first baseman, Gil Hodges. At the other end of the store was Dodgers pitcher Ralph Branca. His line had only two kids waiting on it. Apparently, the Brooklyn faithful had very long memories. They still couldn't get over the home run he gave up to Bobby Thomson in the 1951 playoff game with the Giants.

My dad said to my brother, "Go over there"—he pointed to the much shorter line—"and get that guy's autograph."

My brother said, "I don't want Ralph Branca's autograph."

He wanted his favorite player Gil Hodges's autograph.

My dad responded, "We'll be here all day waiting in that long line. I've got things to do today."

My brother, disappointed, got Ralph Branca's autograph, and they left the store to run some errands. My brother, who was totally disgusted, would eventually throw out that autograph. Too bad my father missed a golden opportunity to make his oldest son happy that day. He had no appreciation of the significance of that event. Autographs meant nothing to him, or he might have gotten Babe Ruth's autograph when he was delivering fish on that golf course.

In 1957, the Dodgers decided to leave Brooklyn for the greener pastures of California. Starting in 1958, they would call Los Angeles their new baseball home.

The New York Giants decided to relocate to San Francisco that same year. Therefore, their ongoing rivalry could continue on the West Coast.

My father and brother were heartbroken since their favorite baseball team was leaving Brooklyn for good. I was only five years old at the time, but I do have a recollection of watching Dodgers baseball games with them in our apartment. I don't recall seeing Duke Snyder or Gil Hodges hitting any game-winning home runs. I do remember hearing Red Barber, with his distinctive Southern drawl, hawking Lucky Strike cigarettes on those Dodgers broadcasts. Maybe that's why I never became a smoker.

With both New York National League teams leaving town, only the hated Yankees remained as the only baseball team in our area. My father and brother could not bring themselves to root for the Yankees. They witnessed the Yankees having defeated the Dodgers in every World Series matchup until 1955. That would be Brooklyn's only World Championship. With mixed emotions, they would follow their baseball heroes' performance from afar. They hated Dodgers owner Walter O'Malley for having taken their team away from Brooklyn. Rooting for the team's success now that they were in California was very difficult. They still loved many of their Dodger heroes who, I'm sure, would have chosen to remain in Brooklyn if it were up to them. Many of those ballplayers made Brooklyn their home in the off season.

My father, brother, and I would have to wait a few years before we could get emotionally involved with another baseball team.

In 1962, National League baseball returned to the New York City area. Through expansion Major League Baseball created two new teams, the New York Mets and the Houston Colt 45s. The Mets would play their first two home seasons in the old Polo Grounds. Their new uniforms would include the old blue and orange colors of the Brooklyn Dodgers and New York Giants. The NY insignia of their baseball caps was the same one used by the old New York Giants. Former Yankee Casey Stengel would become the team's first manager. We were all ecstatic to have a National League team that we could all root for again. The Mets would go on to add many former Dodgers and Giants players to their expansion team in the early years. Unfortunately, these former heroes and all stars were well past their prime when they returned home, but that didn't really matter to us. The "Duke of Flatbush" and Gil Hodges were back home where they belonged.

My father took us to a few baseball games at the Polo Grounds in Upper Manhattan. He purchased my first New York

Mets yearbook in 1962, and I became a Mets fan for life. He even got it autographed by the third string catcher Joe Pignatano, who was a friend of his coworker, attending the game with us. My dad wasn't pleased when I asked Joe if he could get Frank Thomas to autograph it for me.

He was my favorite Met who led the team in home runs and in runs batted in that year. He politely said Frank was busy and handed me my yearbook. My father was so embarrassed. Hey, I was only ten! What did I know? This occasion wouldn't be the last time I said something stupid to a Mets player.

We went to several games at the Polo Grounds over the first two seasons. Old Timers Day and Camera Day were two that stood out to me. On Camera Day, prior to the start of the game, the players would pose for pictures on the perimeter of the playing field. They would do funny things so we could capture that Kodak moment. I have many pictures from that event, including one of my favorite Mets, Frank Thomas. He was a huge man, who picked up the diminutive pitcher Al Jackson like he was a rag doll.

On Old Timers Day, we got great seats right behind home plate. My dad brought along his Bell & Howell 8MM camera and recorded my getting autographs of all the Old Timers sitting in our area. He would tell me who the players were, and for their autograph, I would address them by name. I got ex-Giant Bobby Thomson and ex-Dodger Ralph Branca to sign on the same page of my notebook. I had no idea about how coincidental that was until my father shared the story about "the shot heard 'round the world!" Unlike my brother, I kept and still have Ralph Branca's autograph. Bobby Thomson's home run in 1951 happened the year before I was born.

In 1964, the Mets would move to Shea Stadium, their newly built home in Flushing, Queens. It was named after William Shea, a lawyer, who was instrumental in bringing National

League baseball back to the New York area. New York City Parks Commissioner Robert Moses offered this very same location to Mr. O'Malley before his departure to Los Angeles. Mr. O'Malley said his Brooklyn fans wouldn't travel to Queens to watch his team play. Besides, they were the Brooklyn Dodgers not the Queens Dodgers. I think he was sadly mistaken or had other plans for his Dodgers.

Drawing record crowds, Shea Stadium would become the Mets home field for the next forty-five years. Many, if not all, early fans were Dodgers and Giants faithful. In April 2009, the Mets moved into their new ballpark, Citi Field, which was built on the old Shea Stadium parking lot. Mets' attendance continues to flourish as they have a rabid and loyal fan base. Did Mr. O'Malley really think the Brooklyn fans would hop on an airplane to California to see their team play? Did he keep the name Brooklyn when they moved, or did they become the Los Angeles Dodgers? I guess the new location and Brooklyn name weren't so important anymore after Los Angeles gave him a sweetheart deal which included 300 acres of land and promised funding for access roads for his brand-new stadium.

Farewell to Mr. O'Malley and our beloved "Bums!"

Now for my other embarrassing moment with a Mets player. In 1967, the schoolyard guys decided to take a road trip to James Monroe High School in the Bronx. Several Met players were going to be conducting a baseball clinic for kids our age. Eddie Kranepool, a James Monroe High School graduate, would be leading a group of players, which included Tom Seaver and several other Mets standouts. So excited to see our baseball heroes up close and personal, we took the long train ride to the Bronx from Brooklyn. The event went smoothly until the end when the players conducted a question-and-answer session. Sitting in the gymnasium bleachers, I eagerly raised my hand and was called on by Tom Seaver. I don't recall the exact question I asked, but it went something like, "What were you thinking when you hung that curve ball to Hank Aaron?" This question did not sit well with Tom Terrific. As you could imagine, he went on to lecture me about his pitch selection for that particular at bat. Okay, I wasn't ten years old now; I was fifteen, but I was still a stupid kid. Nevertheless, I didn't hold a grudge against Tom for that heated exchange we experienced that day in the Bronx. I deserved his stern lecture.

I have attended many baseball games at the Polo Grounds, Shea Stadium, and the Mets' current home, Citi Field, over the years. The game that stands out the most to me was October 18, 1986, the opening game of the World Series. I took my dad to see the Mets play the Boston Red Sox. This was the first World Series game he ever attended.

I was lucky enough to get two tickets through a phone lottery system created for that series. Trying repeatedly until I finally connected just after midnight, I dialed into the dedicated phone line to get our tickets. That was the second lottery I had ever won. You will learn about the first lottery later in this book.

On that day, the Mets lost the game 1-0. Mets hurler Ron Darling pitched extremely well only giving up one unearned run over seven innings. Although it was a crushing defeat, it will always remain a fond and cherished memory because of who was sitting next me.

The Mets would go on to capture that World Series by defeating the Red Sox four games to three. Tom Seaver was a member of that losing 1986 Red Sox team. He never pitched in any of the games because he had suffered a knee injury. We did, however, give him a standing ovation during the pre-game introductions. I told you; I didn't hold any grudges.

I have one last note on my Mets fandom. Attending their games (mostly in Philly now), collecting their memorabilia, and being the proud owner of every Mets yearbook going back to their inaugural season in 1962, I remain a devoted New York Mets fan. I never got over not getting Frank Thomas's autograph on that fateful day in the Polo Grounds in 1962. That sad feeling of a missed opportunity stayed with me well into my old age.

One day when I was internet shopping for some more Mets memorabilia, I came across an interesting item. It was a replica of the front cover of the 1962 Mets yearbook autographed by Frank Thomas, Ed Kranepool, and Jay Hook, who was the winning pitcher of the Mets first ever win on April 23, 1962. What a find! I could now have the autographs of my two all-time favorite Mets players, Frank Thomas and Ed Kranepool, with Jay Hook's autograph as the icing on the cake. I suddenly turned into that jubilant ten-year-old kid all over again when I framed that Mets yearbook cover and put it on a wall in my home office. It's my prized possession of all the Mets memorabilia I've collected over the years. It has very little monetary value to sports' enthusiasts, but it's priceless to me.

CHAPTER EIGHT

My Dad, the Dealmaker and TV Repairman

In the mid-1940s, Roy Rogers, Gene Autry, and William "Hopalong Cassidy" Boyd were generally regarded as the most popular B-Western movie cowboys. One Christmas holiday season, my mom asked my dad to pick up a Roy Rogers pistol and holster set for my brother. Prepared to make a deal with the store owner, my dad headed to the toy store. You see, my dad always felt every potential retail purchase should be negotiated. He was never content paying the full retail price for anything. He was always looking for his next big deal. Of course, in most large department and grocery stores, he couldn't put his shrewd negotiating skills to the test. However, he would turn into the Monty Hall of Boro Park with every local merchant he encountered. He would have made a great substitute TV host on the *Let's Make a Deal* show.

When he entered the toy store, he asked about the Roy Rogers pistol and holster set. He was shocked when the store owner revealed the price of that item. My dad asked if there was anything he could do about lowering the price. The owner said it's the suggested retail price a customer would find in any toy or department store.

My dad then asked if the owner had a less expensive version of that pistol and holster set. The owner checked his inventory and returned. He came out with a similar toy pistol and holster set. This was in an open box, which had a Roy Rogers and a Gene Autry gun in it. These guns looked vastly different from one another and didn't match the holster set. He said he could sell my dad this opened box item at a reduced price. My father took that deal. When he got home, my mother asked what Dad had bought.

My father responded, "I got your son a great deal! Now he could boast to his friends that he is the proud owner of two famous cowboys' guns, instead of one."

My mother was furious because she knew when he left the apartment that morning, he wasn't shopping for this mismatched toy gun set. Nonetheless, my father convinced her that my brother would be ecstatic with the purchase he just made. When Christmas arrived and Vinny unwrapped his gift, my mother knew instantly, by the look on his face, that he wasn't a happy cowboy. Yet my dad seemed as indifferent as Monty Hall would have been when a contestant, expecting a new car behind the curtain, got a gag gift like a donkey eating hay instead.

Was there another kid hopping along in Boro Park with a mismatched Roy Rogers and Gene Autry toy gun set just like my brother's? Probably not. My guess is that kid had two Hopalong Cassidy toy pistols in his holster.

My deal-maker father would like to test his negotiating skills with each merchant on the avenue. My parents did most of our clothes shopping along 13th Avenue when we lived in Boro Park. Yet when he needed to make a larger purchase such as a winter overcoat or raincoat for us, we headed over to Orchard Street in Lower Manhattan. There he would really enjoy haggling with all the shop owners on that famous street.

Once my brother and I needed new winter coats. We both decided that this winter season we wanted black leather jackets instead of cloth coats. On our way to Orchard Street, my father plotted his strategy for this next major clothing purchase. I'm sure he felt that he had some negotiating leverage because he was purchasing *two* leather jackets, not just one. Trying on multiple jackets, we would go in and out of stores all day. When we finally found something that fit well and looked good, then the fun would begin. The salesman would say each jacket cost $30.

My father would reply, "My younger son is half the size of his brother. His jacket should be half the price."

The salesman would respond, "That's not how it works sir."

My father would insist that the salesman reduce the price of my jacket or we would be leaving the store. When the salesman took off only five dollars, my father would say, "Boys, take those jackets off, we are going to another store."

And off we would go. The salesman would stop us at the door and say, "Okay, I'll take ten dollars off, but that's all I can do."

My father would respond, "It's not enough. Take *fifteen* dollars off."

This cat-and-mouse game would go on and on. If the final price were not to my father's liking, we would leave the store. This display of gamesmanship went on, up and down Orchard Street. Going clothes shopping with my dad was a totally exhausting and embarrassing experience.

After visiting every store on the street, guess where he would finally purchase our new jackets? Bingo! The very first store we visited. Why? The salesman there had a good while to stew over his lost sales' opportunity. If he had no floor traffic or sales during that time, he felt a smaller profit would be better than none. Also, on Orchard Street, it was considered bad luck not making a sale with one's first morning customer. In all likelihood, the store still made a reasonable profit on the sale after this ordeal. The Monty Hall of Boro Park was very happy *not* to have paid the suggested retail price for our jackets.

With a few more growth spurts in my future, I would be watching my dad play *Let's Make a Deal* on Orchard Street quite a few more times. *I'll take door number three, Monty! Please, Dad, take door number three, and let's get the heck outta here!*

Monty purchased a twelve-inch Zenith TV when television sets first hit the consumer market. He was so excited with his new acquisition. There would be no more gathering around the radio for our in-home family entertainment. Unfortunately, this brand-new invention would have its operational issues. The vacuum tubes behind the large picture tube were constantly burning out. We knew it was time for a tube replacement when we had a distorted picture or poor sound quality. My dad would open up the back of the set, remove all the tubes, and head over to our local pharmacy.

He wasn't making the trip to the pharmacy for any medication or headache remedy. The pharmacy had a TV tube testing machine there. My dad would insert the glass vacuum tubes, which had metal prongs on the bottom, into a matching receptacle on the tube testing machine. It would disclose if the vacuum tube was still operational. When the machine revealed a failing tube, my dad would go over to the pharmacist's counter and purchase a new one. In the 1950s, TV tubes had a very short lifespan. We made quite a few trips to that pharmacy over the years.

We had our twelve-inch Zenith TV for well over ten years. When color TV started showing up in people's homes in the mid 1960s, we wanted to move on to this next generation of televisions. My dad had no problem continuing to make trips to our local pharmacy, since he was on a first name basis with the pharmacist. He finally got tired of our constant complaining and gave in to our new TV demands.

My mother and I accompanied my father on this quest for a brand-new color television set. When we got to the appliance store, the salesman showed us many different TV models of various sizes. The largest color TV he showed us was a twenty-five-inch RCA model. The color picture was beautiful and much larger than that of our tiny black-and-white television in our home. My mother and I were sold. We wanted to purchase this TV. When my father heard the retail sales price, he wanted more buying options to consider. Even moving down in picture size, the cost of a color television was close to three times as much as a comparable black-and-white set. When the salesperson saw my father's hesitation, he tried a different sales approach. He took us to another part of the store featuring the largest TVs made at that time. He showed us a twenty-seven-inch Magnavox TV in a beautiful wooden cabinet. My mom and I thought this step up in size was crazy. Twenty-seven inches would be like having a movie theatre screen in our apartment. There was, however, one small catch with this massive TV. It was a black-and-white model. Did this deter my pop from buying it? Heck no! He would tell us that, if we made this purchase, we would have the largest TV in all of Boro Park. Everyone would be knocking down our doors to witness the largest television sold in the country. He then proceeded to purchase that twenty-seven-inch, black-and-white Magnavox TV for our future viewing pleasure.

 I'm pretty confident that the sales price of this model compared to that of the twenty-five-inch RCA color model had absolutely nothing to do with his final decision. He talked himself into thinking that this was one of his best deals ever. After we arrived at home with our new TV, which was a major size upgrade from our old Zenith, we were still disappointed. We would now be stuck in this black-and-white world for a number of years while most people would be enjoying their TV viewing in Technicolor. My friends would boast about observing the majestic green baseball fields or the beautiful outdoor scenery on TV shows like *Bonanza*. I complained to my father that this purchase was going to haunt us for years. Nevertheless, he remained steadfast in his position.

One day, he brought home what he thought would be a solution to my TV-viewing woes. Was it a new color television set? Nope! He brought home a multi-colored plastic sheet that we could adhere to the glass of our black-and-white TV screen. This rainbow on plastic was his solution to my color-TV issues. In his mind, he had just converted our large black-and-white television set to a color set with this one simple fix. It was great if we didn't mind watching purple grass on the playing fields or Little Joe and Hoss Cartwright with green faces. That plastic rainbow purchase quickly made its way to the trash can after we all got dizzy watching television.

CHAPTER NINE

A Tree Falls in Brooklyn

In 1955, my father traded in his old Buick for a 1952 Pontiac Chieftain. It was a beautiful two-toned green car. My dad never bought a brand-new car in his life. He always felt he could get more value with a car that was at least two or three years old. One drawback with his car-buying logic was that although he did save some money, his cars already had some wear and tear and mileage on them. He was very protective of their longevity by not wanting to drive them for vacations as they aged. My mother wanted to capitalize on his latest purchase by taking a little vacation before this car went into hibernation.

Regardless of the timing of any of his used car purchases, my dad did not like to drive on his days off. He would tell my mother that he drove all the time for a living, and he needed a break from it. When that excuse wore thin, he would then say his old cars were unreliable, and he didn't want to get stuck far away from home. Taking away the reliability concerns he would predictably raise soon, my mother needed to act quickly. Besides, she was also looking for a little diversity in our lives as our only traveling involved going to and from one relative to another. Living in a small apartment and working in a sweatshop five days a week, my mother was looking for a little adventure for herself and her kids.

She finally convinced my dad into taking a short trip to Lake George in Upstate New York. They planned on leaving Brooklyn when my dad got home from work on a Friday afternoon. The mini vacation plan was to return home Sunday after spending two nights in Lake George.

On Friday afternoon, August 12, 1955, we packed our bags and headed off to Upstate New York. On the car ride there, we were discussing all the plans we had for the upcoming weekend. Boat rides on the lake, sightseeing, visiting museums, and eating at fancy restaurants were some of the items on our short vacation itinerary. When we arrived in Lake George, the skies opened up with a torrential rain, which confined us to our motel room the rest of the day. We escaped briefly to eat dinner, then returned to our motel room. Now being soaking wet from that eating experience, my father started complaining that this trip had been a mistake. He argued that had we stayed home, we all wouldn't have been cooped up in a small motel room. He wanted to go back to Brooklyn that night.

My mother said, "Let's see how the weather is tomorrow before making any hasty decisions."

The next morning the rain continued to fall even harder, with more force than that of the day before.

My dad said, "We are not spending the entire weekend in this motel room. Pack your stuff, we are heading home."

Not surprisingly, our short weekend vacation in Lake George came to an abrupt end. We headed back to Brooklyn after breakfast. Making our return trip much slower and hazardous, the rain seemed to follow us all the way back home. My dad lamented in the car that this lost weekend should have never happened. He had never wanted to go to Lake George in the first place. His gut feeling was to remain in Boro Park; he should have followed his instincts. Upon arriving home, he parked his car in his usual location on 58th Street, just off the corner of 14th Avenue. We all retreated to our apartment building entrance, and our short vacation was officially over. What wasn't over was the continued downpour we witnessed in Brooklyn that day. On Saturday,

August 13, 1955, Hurricane Connie, producing extremely high winds, came through Boro Park with a total rainfall of 13.24 inches. The next morning, a neighbor knocked on our apartment door informing us that a large tree was uprooted and had crashed through the roof of our new car. We all went downstairs to see what had happened. Just as the neighbor said, our car had been the landing spot for a large fallen tree on 58th Street. My father's beautiful two-toned green Pontiac wasn't looking so good at that moment. Dad ran upstairs to get his camera to take pictures of the damage. He then contacted his insurance company to file a claim. To his surprise, the insurance agent told him there wasn't any record of his new vehicle. Apparently, my father had forgotten to transfer his old policy to his new car.

The company representative stated that the claim couldn't be honored since only the Buick had been insured. Of course, the Monty Hall of Boro Park was having none of that. He called and spoke to numerous individuals at the insurance company over the next few days. His argument was that all his previous vehicles had been insured with that company. He was current with his insurance coverage payments and a mistake of one week should not disqualify him from making that claim. He finally got a representative to agree with him, and his claim was honored. The car was fully restored, and we had our wheels back on the road. This time, Monty picked the right curtain and got back his new car instead of that straw-eating donkey.

CHAPTER TEN

The Holidays

Although we visited with all of our family and paisanos from Sicily on a regular basis, the year-end holidays were almost always spent with Aunt Millie, Uncle Bennie, and my cousins on Long Island. Holiday gatherings were becoming more challenging as my Brooklyn and New Jersey cousins were getting older and starting to have families of their own. When we did entertain for the holidays, my father would break out a large folding table, which he would set up in our parlor. We barely had room for our families to sit on a couch after a meal. Having two families in one room was a bit too close for comfort. As we got older, we would eventually spend more time on Long Island during the holidays. When we moved into our Gravesend home, we were able to accommodate more people and began to alternate holidays again.

We could always look forward to plenty of good food, laughter, and joy at these special times of the year. My mom and aunt were in charge of the kitchen area. My father would supply the seven fishes for our special Christmas Eve dinner. I always knew that the holidays were fast approaching when I would find live lobsters draped in wet towels in the vegetable drawer of our fridge. It seemed like when I opened the refrigerator door, a lobster claw would try to close it.

My dad would also have crabs, scallops, swordfish, shrimp, mussels, and calamari, as I remember. The meal may have seemed like a real feast for fish connoisseurs, but for me, the dinner was a real nightmare. Maybe growing up with the abundance of fish my father brought home, I became a little turned off to those little underwater creatures. Following the Catholic church directive of not eating meat on Fridays, we always had some kind of fish on the menu. Not until 1966, when the church pulled back on that form of penance, did I finally get to see a hot dog or hamburger on a Friday. To appease this little brat on Christmas Eve, Aunt Millie would make a casserole of eggplant parmigiana especially for me. Most Italians would say, "You gave up the seven fishes for eggplant? Are you crazy?" Don't answer that question! I had to also put up with Uncle Bennie chiding me about my food preferences. I would always get lines such as, "Taste this baked clam, you'll love it," or "Try this fish; it tastes just like chicken." The last comment would always be, "You don't know what you're missing!" This banter, too, like the seven fishes, would also become a Christmas Eve family tradition that I had to endure for many years. The family really freaked out when I declared that I was becoming a full-fledged vegetarian. I'll leave that story for another day.

One of the things I really looked forward to during the holiday season was playing table games with my family.

Besides the traditional Italian card games, the older folks liked to play, we would try some of the new board games that were being introduced during the holidays. My cousin Annette was somehow put in charge of keeping us up to date with the latest games. There was always something to look forward to after our hearty meal and multiple desserts. As for the desserts, we did purchase the traditional Italian cookies and pastries, but the homemade desserts were my favorites on the holidays. Cream puffs, cookies, cheesecake, and my aunt's famous flan were treats we favored over store-bought items.

The last and best part of our Christmas Eve was exchanging gifts, especially when they were distributed by Santa himself. I purchased a Santa Claus costume one year when our kids were very young. We alternated who would wear the costume to throw off the kids. One year, it was my cousin Albert's turn to play Santa Claus. His experience as Jolly Saint Nick was a little different than the others who donned that Santa suit. All gifts were wrapped and placed in large black garbage bags located in the garage. Unfortunately, when this Santa came upstairs with his first bag of gifts, he mistakenly took a real bag of garbage along with him. I will never forget the look on the kids' faces when he pulled out his first gift, and it was an empty can of breadcrumbs! Santa did a lot of ho-ho-ho-ing with that bag of Christmas gifts and provided a cherished memory our family would never forget.

CHAPTER ELEVEN

Coney Island

In 1963, the 58th Street gang took its first (and my only) road trip to Steeplechase Park in Coney Island. My friends and I weren't old enough to travel the subways without adult supervision. Elena was one member of our gang whose older sister Carol volunteered to supervise our day trip. Steeplechase Park was one of three amusement parks on Coney Island. The other two were Ward's Kiddie Park and Astroland. Of the three, Steeplechase Park was our preferred destination. We were too old for the kiddie park, and Astroland required us to buy individual tickets for each ride located there.

At Steeplechase Park, we bought a circular ticket, which had thirteen little printed circles around its edge. Each ticket came with a string to be placed around the neck. We gained entry to rides and attractions after the attendant punched a hole into one of the circles. A funny face of a man called Tillie, with several dozen teeth, whom I later realized was a caricature of George C. Tilyou, the park's founder, was dead center on this hole punch ticket. We felt as if we were getting a real bargain by not having to pay for each ride individually as Astroland required. Steeplechase had simpler, comedic rides where Astroland had more elaborate, larger rides and attractions.

Steeplechase Park did, however, have one of the largest attractions in Coney Island with its Parachute Jump. This ride was relocated to Steeplechase Park in 1941 from Flushing Meadow, Queens, home of the 1939 New York World's Fair. Although the ride was still in operation when we got there, none of us had the guts to tackle that monster. We probably wouldn't have met the height requirement if we had attempted to get on that ride. We did, however, enjoy other rides and attractions in the park, especially the Steeplechase Race.

The Steeplechase Race had riders mounting wooden horses and racing each other on metal tracks with the power of gravity behind them. The horses would travel at a good pace on a very long and winding course. The ride tried to create the illusion of that of a real horse race.

Although Steeplechase had many of the same rides that would be found in other amusement parks like the Sports Car Ride, Tilt-a-Whirl, and Round-Up, the Steeplechase Race was the most fun and memorable ride that we still reminisce about to this day. No, I don't remember what place I finished in our horse race. I just remember how much fun we had on those wooden horses.

In 1964 Steeplechase Park closed its doors for good, and Coney Island amusement park enthusiasts were left with Astroland and many individual rides along Surf Avenue to get their death-defying thrills.

There were three rides I had to go on every time I visited Coney Island. They were the Cyclone roller coaster, the Wonder Wheel, and the Bobsled.

Built in 1927, the Cyclone was a wooden roller coaster that reached a top speed of 60 miles per hour on its 2,640-foot track. Noted for its 85-foot vertical drop at a 58.6-degree descent angle, the Cyclone was the world's second-steepest wooden roller coaster. I always thought the front seat was the scariest because there was nothing obstructing your view of what was coming, but my friends had different opinions. Some of them thought the back seat was worse because you couldn't see what was coming and your body would be thrown violently from side to side. Both scared the crap out of me! The rickety wooden structure vibrated and shook as the car sped on the tracks, making us fear the coaster would fly off the rails and onto the Coney Island beach. However, my friends and I were not deterred from going on that ride repeatedly. To this day, some ninety years after the coaster was built, it is still considered one of the best roller coasters in the country.

Built in 1920, the Wonder Wheel was a unique Ferris wheel with both moving and stationary cars. The moving cars thrilled riders by traveling back and forth on tracks, giving the illusion that they might fly off the ride. Stationary cars, on the other hand, provided a calmer experience for those who wanted a bird's-eye view of the park and beach below. As you might guess, I always opted for the moving cars.

The Bobsled roller coaster, like the Parachute Jump, was initially constructed for the 1939 World's Fair and relocated to Coney Island in 1941. Its distinctive track was designed to mimic an actual bobsled run. Riders would speed through partially enclosed wooden tubes with open tops, banking high on curves and nearly flipping upside down. The ride offered all the thrills of a bobsled run, minus the snow, ice, and cold. Maybe because Steeplechase closed in the fall and reopened in the spring.

There were other roller coasters I enjoyed in Coney Island during those days. The ones I vividly remember were the Thunderbolt, Tornado, and the single-car coaster called the Wild Mouse. All were fun, exciting rides, but none of them could hold a candle to the thrilling Cyclone roller coaster.

The New York City Landmarks Preservation Commission has designated the Parachute Jump, Cyclone Roller Coaster, and Wonder Wheel as landmarks.

How could one write about Coney Island without mentioning Nathan's Famous. Founded by Nathan Handwerker and his wife, Ida Handwerker, in 1916, they sold their nickel hot dogs from a stand that still exists today at its original site on the corner of Surf and Stillwell Avenues. My friends and I would sometimes travel to Coney Island just to go to Nathan's for lunch or dinner. Imagine going to Coney Island just to eat a meal and bypassing the amusement parks and beach?

Eating a hot dog at Nathan's Famous was certainly worth the trip. Their hot dogs and crinkle cut french fries were the best Brooklyn had to offer. The owners had plenty of other items on the menu back then, but I sampled only one other. That was Nathan's chow mein sandwich. Sounds crazy, but Nathan's served chow mein on a hamburger bun with deep fried noodles dripping with gravy. It was to die for, when I was a kid.

When we didn't feel like making the trip to Nathan's Famous in Coney Island, we went to Big Daddy's restaurant in Sheepshead Bay on Coney Island Avenue. Their hot dogs were a close second to Nathan's Famous back in the day. Perhaps because the restaurant founders were Robert "Big Daddy" Napp and Murray L. Handwerker, nephew of Nathan Handwerker, founder of Nathan's Famous. Big Daddy's had a food menu similar to Nathan's, including the chow mein sandwich. One distinct difference between the two places was the decor of Big Daddy's, which had red-and-white candy-striped walls with pictures of big-time celebrities and Robert "Big Daddy" Napp placed throughout the restaurant. Unfortunately, Big Daddy's Brooklyn location closed in 1977. Their last location in South Beach, Florida, closed sometime in 1991.

Nathan's Famous would go on to open many locations and distribute hot dogs in over 65,000 supermarket and grocery locations in the United States. They stopped serving the chow mein sandwich in 2010.

I can't wait to sample one of their new meatless hot dogs.

CHAPTER TWELVE

Catholic School

I guess you could say my mother was very overprotective of me maybe because of that Sparky incident or maybe because she was just a little crazy. Whatever her reasoning, instead of going to kindergarten with all the other kids my age, I spent another supposed beneficial year at home with Zia Alfia. In my opinion that decision would prove to be an error in judgment. It further enhanced my mama's boy condition, which possibly stunted my personal growth and may explain why I entered the first grade at St. Frances de Chantal kicking and screaming like a lunatic.

Most of my first-grade classmates had attended kindergarten in a public school. Already having had a year out of their nest, they could fly freely. I, with Zia Alfia as my only friend, felt completely isolated and out of place in school and needed time to assimilate with this group of kids. In those days, the school was predominately run by the Sisters of the Dominican Order and a few lay teachers. A lay teacher, my first-grade instructor possibly made my transition to the classroom a little easier, for lay teachers were not as intimidating as the Dominican nuns in that school. After getting over the initial shock of separation from my mother and Zia, I would eventually adjust to being in school, all day, every day. Like most well-adjusted kids, I would go on to attend grades one through five without any incidents.

I was on my way to the good Catholic education my parents had hoped for. However, that peace and tranquility all ended when I reached the sixth grade. Then my world would be turned upside down when I had the good fortune of being assigned to a class instructed by a nun who I will refer to as Sister X. Sister X was a mean-spirited, creepy individual who seemed to take great joy in inflicting harm and pain on some of her students.

Many of the nuns in that school were pleasant for the most part, but a few ruled with an iron fist. I know; fifty-plus kids in a classroom, with no aids to assist them, was a tough assignment for any sane human being. While most were able to cope with the classroom size, Sister X had a demented and evil way of keeping order in her classroom. If classmates weren't ducking erasers thrown at their heads or getting smacked on their knuckles with a metal ruler, our teacher was probably on her medications or out sick that day. She gave a whole new meaning to the phrase "duck and cover," actions which were drills we used to practice in case we were under nuclear attack from the Soviet Union. Those drills came in handy when Sister X was erasing the chalkboard.

Apparently, she took great pride in humiliating eleven-year-olds, especially the eleven-year-old boys in her class. She would make crazy statements: "I see the children in the first two rows are talking and laughing. Can those two rows please stand and form a line to the right of me?"

She would then grab a long wooden pointer (which she rarely used for educational purposes) and began to whack each one of us on the backside as we leaned over her desk. I must admit it really didn't hurt that much, but getting whacked in front of fifty of one's peers was a totally humiliating experience. To make matters worse, I was never talking in those rows when, at least on those occasions, she would call us out. I almost forgot to mention she possessed a cat o' nine tails. This was a multi-tailed whip or flail she kept on her desk. I never saw her hit a student with it, but she did pick it up and wrap it against her desk a few times to get our attention. Think about that for a second. Where would a "woman of the cloth" purchase a cat o' nine tails in 1963? Maybe she hung out with a gang in Greenwich Village on her days off. I do know one thing for sure: she definitely didn't buy it on Amazon.

The entire Catholic school experience had really worn me down at that point. Some of these nuns would have made excellent SS Officers under Heinrich Himmler of the Third Reich. "You *vill* listen! You *vill* be quiet!"

There was no talking as we lined up in the schoolyard. Students couldn't speak in the hallways or stairwells, had to march silently from the classroom to mass, and remain quiet while in church. Of course, as you know, students couldn't speak in class, especially in the first two rows of Sister X's class. This silent society was the kiss of death for a little gabby kid who loved to talk all the time.

Watching kids sobbing in the stairwells, because a hall monitor pulled them out for talking, was pitiful to witness every day. They would whimper, "I don't want to see Sister Monica; please don't take me to Sister Monica." The assistant principal and official disciplinarian of our school was Sister Monica. The rumor was she had a spanking machine in her office. That turned out to be a very large wooden paddle. All this nonsense took its toll on me physically and mentally. I would wake up every morning with a severe stomachache. I didn't want to go to that school anymore. My parents brought me to see a specialist to find out what was causing my gastrointestinal issues. I could have saved them the time and money because Sister X was the cause of my emotional and physical pain.

Desperate to get me out of my funk, my parents even purchased a little puppy for me. I wished it had been a German shepherd that could have accompanied me to school. There was no such thing as service animals in those days, even a German shepherd who the SS Officers might have identified with. Since that wasn't in the cards, my parents had to try something else.

They set up a meeting with the school principal and Sister X to see if they could resolve all my emotional issues. In the principal's office, the two nuns seemed deeply compassionate and concerned for my well-being. They assured my parents that they would address my problems. At this meeting, Sister X seemed to transform into Saint X, a very caring and loving individual.

I was truly witnessing her epiphany without her having experienced the process of canonization. I had witnessed a true miracle from above. As we left the office, Sister X took me by the hand, down the hallway, into the elevator. Completing their discussion, my parents remained near the principal's office.

As the elevator doors were closing, Sister X grabbed me by the ear, nearly lifting me off the floor. She said, "If you ever tell your parents again about what goes on in our classroom, there will be hell to pay."

So much for that heavenly intervention I had just witnessed in the principal's office. Then we walked into the classroom, and to my amazement, she brought me to the front of the room and proclaimed, "Everyone, let's welcome Thomas back to our class; he's feeling much better now."

That was the final nail in the coffin for me. Totally mortified, with my newly acquired cauliflower ear, I decided I was never stepping foot in that school again. How was I to convince my parents that I was dealing with a Psycho Sister? Luckily, out of the corner of his eye, my father saw Sister X lifting me off the elevator floor by my ear. When I got home and started to tell him my story, he interrupted me and said he had witnessed what had happened. After months of having told my parents what a nut job this lady was, he finally saw for himself that I wasn't fabricating this story.

Not long after that fiasco, we moved from Boro Park to the Gravesend section of Brooklyn. After twenty years of marriage, my parents would finally own their first home. Something really good resulted from my Catholic school experience with Norman Bates, err, Sister X.

I got a puppy, my brother and I got our own rooms, and it was *"Hasta la vista, baby!"* to that Castro Convertible forever!

For the record, I didn't use Sister X's real name in this book because I have permanently deleted it from my memory bank. It might have been Sister Catherine the Witch, or Sister Catherine of the Third Reich, but don't hold me to that. My not disclosing her real name certainly wasn't to protect her since she is probably long gone from this earth as is the St. Frances de Chantal elementary school. Good riddance to them both! I know, I know, I'm going to rot in Hell for having written this chapter, but take a wild guess who will be greeting me at the front gate?

CHAPTER THIRTEEN

Almost Jersey Bound

Before settling into our new home in the Gravesend section of Brooklyn, my parents had been considering all of their home-buying options. We looked at homes in Queens and along the Nassau County border of Long Island. We also took trips to New Jersey to look at new housing developments near the tunnels and bridges. My father, who worked in Lower Manhattan, didn't want to venture too far from his comfort zone. Making his daily fish deliveries, he was already logging in many driving miles at work. He didn't need to compound the problem by extending his traveling any further than his current Boro Park commute.

Uncle Benny and Aunt Dolly had recently relocated from the Lower East Side of New York to Rutherford, New Jersey. Like my dad, Uncle Benny also worked in the Fulton Fish Market. He told him that his commute was fairly reasonable and that the travel time would be similar to my father's commute from Brooklyn. Their Rutherford development had new homes being built right next door to them. We took a ride there one weekend. My parents liked the area and were impressed with the models and floor plans they saw. In fact, they were so impressed they put a down payment on a new home.

Suddenly, the realization that I would be leaving Brooklyn forever to become a Jersey boy hit me like a ton of bricks. I loved my aunt, uncle, and cousins, but a relocation of this magnitude would be totally life altering for me. On the ride home I decided to share my feelings with my parents. They listened and then said they were committed to making this move for the benefit of my brother and myself. I'm not exactly sure how my eighteen-year-old brother felt about leaving Brooklyn, but this eleven-year-old was not in favor of the move. As we continued on our drive home, I wasn't making any headway with a civil discussion. As a result, I decided to escalate matters by crying and screaming my opinion for the remainder of the trip home. I cried so loud and long that I severely damaged my vocal cords. When we arrived back home in Boro Park, I had no voice whatsoever. I could barely get a whisper out. My inability to speak would continue for days.

My parents became so concerned they took me to see our family physician. He referred us to a laryngologist, who specialized in vocal cords and care of the voice. He concluded that my screaming had created polyps on my vocal cords. His recommendation was that I shouldn't speak for a couple of weeks so that my vocal cords could possibly heal. If that approach proved to be ineffective, surgery would be my next option. Imagine this loudmouth being told he couldn't talk or utter any words for several weeks. Ouch! This diagnosis scared the bejeebers out of my parents. It also made them reconsider moving to New Jersey.

The next day, they withdrew their offer on the home they had selected in Rutherford. Their decision was music to my ears, which were still in working order at that time.

If this New Jersey episode had not transpired as it had, my brother and I might have had totally different lives. We certainly would have attended different schools. We would have made different friends and acquaintances. Our dating experiences would have been different. We'd probably have different wives and children. Our careers and Armed Service choices might have been different. And for me, my Brooklyn life experience would have ended at age eleven. I am convinced that I would have been a totally different person had I left Brooklyn at that time of my life. My Brooklyn persona would be further developed by remaining in that community and social environment for another sixteen years.

I'm confident that at age eleven I could not have known the profound effect and significance of my actions. Perhaps my having acted as a big baby on that car ride home changed the direction of our lives forever. As my story unfolds one might have a better understanding of my feelings about remaining in Brooklyn. Besides, who would want to read a book about growing up in Rutherford, New Jersey?

CHAPTER FOURTEEN

Meet the Beatles

Like many other eleven-year-olds at the time, I was very excited about seeing the new English rock group called the Beatles. WMCA in New York was the first local radio station in our area to play one of their songs. Disc Jockey Jack Spector, an original "Good Guy" on that station played, "I Want to Hold Your Hand" on December 26, 1963. It became a number-one hit on the Billboard Hot 100 on February 1, 1964. I had purchased their "Meet the Beatles" album when it was released in January 1964. They were scheduled to appear on *The Ed Sullivan Show* on Sunday, February 9, 1964. I was looking forward to seeing what these blokes from Liverpool looked like in person. I would get this opportunity days before the rest of the country.

On February 7, Beatlemania reached John F. Kennedy International Airport, marking the beginning of the British Invasion. Uncle Bennie was a Port Authority police officer stationed at that airport at that time. He was on duty that day and arranged for my dad, my cousin Annette, and me to attend the welcoming event. He positioned his squad car near the aircraft's stairway with the hope of an introduction. Attracting over 3,000 fans who congregated at the airport to observe from windows and viewing platforms, this event was widely covered by the news media.

My cousin and I were ecstatic about our prime position for this once-in-a-lifetime happening. We were so excited to get to the airport that my dad forgot his camera. I didn't care at the time. I was just focused on shaking hands with Paul, John,

George, and Ringo. As the plane arrived and the door opened, my cousin and I were ready to jump out of the police car and meet the Beatles.

Suddenly, my dad shouted, "You kids stay right here!"

We both looked at him and asked, "Why?"

He replied, "They are coming from England, and they may have an infectious disease."

I guess he was thinking back on his 1920 trip through Ellis Island, where immigrants underwent medical inspections before entering the country. And with that, my cousin and I stayed seated in the police car as the Beatles walked right past us. I don't even remember if they looked our way; they were probably focused on the thousands of screaming fans on the international arrivals building observation deck. Another golden opportunity missed. If only I had my Kodak Instamatic camera!

At least I still have my "Meet the Beatles" album, which would have been a collector's item if I hadn't drawn green beards on the faces of the Fab Four.

I did have a history of bad decisions with collectibles. After my dad purchased my 1962 Mets yearbook, I cut the team photo out of it and placed it on the back of my fish tank. I wanted Goldie to have something to look at.

CHAPTER FIFTEEN

Our New Home in Gravesend

Our first Brooklyn home was on Quentin Road between East 3rd and East 4th Streets. Ours was a modest semi-attached home. Compared to our little apartment in Boro Park, it seemed palatial. Three bedrooms with a full bath, a living room, dining room, eat-in kitchen, and soon-to-be finished basement with a half bath made us all giddy. Before relocating to our new house, we all participated in prepping the house for our future occupancy. We cleaned, painted, and discarded the prior owners' unwanted possessions. Carrying small and breakable items, we also made several trips to and from our apartment. My parents didn't trust the movers with a few delicate items, especially our religious statues. This relocation was really starting to sink in with me now. After having heard discussions about home ownership my entire life, this property acquisition was truly becoming a reality for our family.

On one of our trips my father decided he wanted to paint his new workshop. It was a small, windowless room in our basement. After having prepped the walls and ceiling, we began to paint. My mother was cleaning in the kitchen upstairs while my brother was at work. My father used an oil-based paint that had some interesting ingredients in it. Not too long into our painting, we both started laughing uncontrollably.

Everything we said made us both hysterical. The longer we continued to paint, the more disoriented we became. My mother, hearing the commotion, came down the stairs to investigate. She immediately knew something was terribly wrong because we had never laughed like such idiots before. She figured out what had happened and escorted us out of the house, into our common driveway. All the way up our basement stairs and into the driveway we continued to laugh.

My mother kept screaming, "Keep it down!" so our new neighbors wouldn't think some drunken fools had just moved in next door. As I had previously mentioned in my Murray's pushcart story, she was always concerned about people's perceptions of us.

After breathing some fresh air, my father and I began to regain our senses. My dad seemed very embarrassed by this painting episode and how it had affected the both of us. I, on the other hand, got a real kick out of it. How couldn't I? How many people could say that their first experience getting high took place with their old man?

Some of the fondest memories I recall were waking up on Sunday mornings to the sweet aroma of fresh marinara sauce simmering on the stove. Remember it's *sauce*, not *gravy*! Meatballs and sausage would be frying in another pan. Mario Lanza or the Ink Spots would be serenading my parents in the background on their newly purchased hi-fi stereo system. It was a typical Sunday morning experience that my parents seemed to enjoy in their new home.

They would send Daisy upstairs to wake me up around noon for our 2 p.m. lunch. I was a late sleeper in those days. She would run up the stairs, jump on my bed, and scratch my back as if she were digging for a bone. She scratched me so hard that I had no choice but to get out of bed. Let's see Rin Tin Tin or Lassie do that trick!

After lunch, my dad, brother, and I would retreat to the living room and watch a football, baseball or basketball game. Around 4 p.m., my mom would make the espresso coffee and place some desserts and fruit on the dining room table. Then around 6 or 6:30 p.m., my mom would put out a light dinner, which consisted of Italian bread, cheeses, pepperoni, and dried sausage. Ours was a perfect Italian Sunday experience. I truly miss it.

One of the unexpected benefits of having had our own home was the extra living space my brother and I now enjoyed. When we lived in the apartment, some of my parents' paisanos and *famiglia* would stop over on a Saturday or Sunday morning just to say hello and have a cup of coffee. Rather than an entire family, only an uncle or male friend would visit. Let me remind you again that Italians like to visit.

With all that Sicilian chatter going on in the kitchen next to us, it was impossible remaining asleep on that Castro convertible. Now with our bedrooms upstairs, we were insulated from the noise and banter of their weekend visitors.

My brother and I were thrilled with our new living arrangement. Vinny was playing weeknight and weekend gigs with his band. He would get home at all hours of the night. The entire family wouldn't be awakened when he arrived home. He could sleep later in his own room and bed on the weekends because now visitors had use of our couch downstairs. I could also sleep later on the weekends because I wouldn't be awakened by visitors going in and out of our apartment. Our newfound privacy was a marvelous thing.

The larger living space now afforded me the opportunity to invite friends to our home for some fun and games. In Boro Park, I was never able to reciprocate with all the wonderful things I experienced in my friends' homes. Being a host as opposed to a guest was something I always longed for.

My mom and dad enjoyed having their extra living space also. My mother had a roomier kitchen with a large, adjacent dining room. Without breaking out that darn folding table, she could entertain and enjoy family gatherings. In our basement, she enjoyed the convenience of her own washing machine, a significant upgrade from using a washboard in our tub. She happily hung our clothes out to dry in our backyard instead of four stories high. Even though her feet were now on the ground, she was in heaven.

My dad got to enjoy the backyard, too. In Brooklyn most homes had very small backyards. We would refer to them as being a postage stamp-sized yard. Although it wasn't very large, my father got the most out of it. In the rear of the yard, he had two large fig trees. Between the trees, he had his vegetable garden. Every season it would be filled with tomatoes, zucchini, string beans, peppers, basil, and any other vegetable he had decided to grow. At the behest of my mother, who loved seeing her flowers from our kitchen window, the fences along each side of the yard were lined with different color rose bushes. The center of the yard was filled with grass and a small tree. My dad got the most out of this small piece of land with plenty of fruits, vegetables, and flowers occupying almost every square inch available.

Even Daisy benefited from our new surroundings. The house gave her more space to roam. When she wasn't running around the house, we could find her sitting on a ledge in our living room and looking out our large window onto the street. She would be entertained watching people and animals pass by. Her favorite part of the day occurred when the mailman delivered our mail through our front door mail slot. Daisy would jump off the ledge and meet him at the front door as the mail came through the slot. My family needed quick reflexes to be ready for that daily delivery, or our mail would have been shredded into a million pieces. We did use her from time to time to shred documents with our personal information on them. We had a canine paper shredding machine, which made us way ahead of our time.

Besides her indoor fun, Daisy got to spend much more time outdoors at our new home. We could let her stay in our gated backyard with us while she fetched clothespins or merely caught some rays. Now I didn't have to be so concerned with my throwing accuracy. There was no chance of her leaping over the side of a building to chase one of my errant throws. The worst thing that could happen to her would be picking up a few thorns from my mother's rose bushes.

CHAPTER SIXTEEN

The New Block(s)

My new block was now East 3rd Street between Quentin Road and Kings Highway. My new best friend was Glenn, who lived on East 3rd Street with his parents, along with his sister and brother, Ellen and Richard. Glenn would invite me to his house to play his favorite board game "Challenge the Yankees." Having been a big Yankee fan, he would always manage the Yankees, and I would manage the National League All Stars. His team consisted of players including Whitey Ford, Yogi Berra, Roger Maris, and Mickey Mantle. My team featured players like catcher Del Crandall. Although he was an eleven time All-Star, he had a lifetime batting average of .254 with only 179 home runs. Needless to say, Glenn and his Yankees won almost every contest at his dining room table. I didn't really care because I had a new friend who would go on to introduce me to the rest of the gang on East 3rd Street. Marc, Alan, David, Rochelle, Angela, Theresa, and Donna were on that block.

When Glenn and I weren't playing his baseball board game, we listened to our 45s and traded them as if they were baseball cards. I still have a few of his old records with his name printed on them, as I'm sure he has a few of mine.

When our indoor activities concluded, we would join the East 3rd Street gang on the block for outside activities like Stoopball, Boxball, Hit the Penny, Johnny on the Pony, Ringolevio, and Hide-and-Seek. Filled with many interesting characters such as

THE NEW BLOCK(S)

Marc, the block's rogue daredevil, who would gladly accept any crazy challenge, the new block was lots of fun.

One time the gang was getting on the EL on McDonald Avenue and Kings Highway to go to Rockaway Playland. There was no direct train from our station to Rockaway Beach. When going past the Howard Beach station in Queens, we had to pay a double fare to reach the Rockaway peninsula, which was considered a double-fare zone. For some unknown reason, Marc decided he wasn't going to pony up another fifteen cents for the last leg of our trip. The rest of us purchased our tokens and got on the new platform. Marc surveyed the landscape and decided to scale a very high fence to gain entrance to the new platform. We all looked on in amazement as he risked his life to avoid paying another fifteen cents for a token. The East 3rd Street gang got to see a superhero in the making. I'm not sure Spider-Man himself would have found the courage to climb that high fence. Somehow Marc safely reached the train's platform, and we were on our way to Rockaway Playland after having witnessed one the craziest death-defying acts in my life.

Back on East 3rd, Glenn and I were a lot more grounded than our friend Marc. We liked to take bike rides in our neighborhood. We would go to Mangano's Bicycle shop on Avenue U to check out the new bikes that had arrived, or bring our old ones in for repair. We would go to L&B's Spumoni Gardens on 86th Street for a slice of pizza and some Italian ices or just ride up and down Ocean Parkway until we got tired. We would also travel to nearby Bensonhurst on Kings Highway between West 9th and West 11th Streets. There we would find two slot car racing stores, the Thunderbird and Eddie's, both of which had slot car racing tracks running throughout their large stores. Glenn and I preferred Eddie's for our slot car racing. For a quarter, we had use of their racing tracks for one hour. Slot cars were also available to rent if needed.

Slot cars and tracks were expensive to purchase in the sixties and also required a great amount of space for adequate enjoyment. I had my very own HO scale racing set with cars and tracks, which were set up in my basement. The HO cars and tracks were roughly half the size of the traditional slot car arrangement. HO scale racing was a fun hobby but extremely difficult to manage. The smaller cars' speed made keeping the cars from flying off the tracks virtually impossible. That was inconsequential to me since I had a racing track in my basement, and there was no rental fee of twenty-five cents per hour to use it.

One time, Glenn and I traveled out of our neighborhood and decided to take a long ride to my old stomping grounds in Boro Park. I missed my old friends and felt the need to see them again. We rode along Avenue P on to 60th Street all the way back toward my old block, 58th Street. We passed places I used to frequent like the Maple Lanes Bowling Alley. I was so excited to share my old neighborhood experiences with my new friend Glenn. When we reached our final destination on 58th Street, we ran into Tommy and the gang.

The visit was pleasant and cordial, but I got a sense that things had somehow changed. I don't know if they had moved on without me or, as the old saying goes, you can't go home again. They later visited my new home and though we had enjoyed the day, our paths would never cross again until Tommy reached out to me almost fifty years later on Facebook. We exchanged photos and even an 8mm film of my birthday party that he and his sister Liz had attended. It was so nice to reconnect with an old friend whom I shared so many Brooklyn memories with.

Returning to Gravesend, I ventured onto East 4th Street between Quentin Road and Kings Highway where I would make additional friends Chris, Joey, Henry, Hal, Jonathan, and Ronny. At some point while hanging out with Chris and Joey, I became

THE NEW BLOCK(S)

interested in playing music again. Chris played the guitar, Joey the drums.

When I was ten and living in Boro Park, my parents took me for guitar lessons. The teacher had taught my brother how to play years earlier so they figured he could do the same for me. I had a good ear for music but little tolerance for practice repetition and reading sheet music.

The teacher would play a song on his guitar, and I would replicate it on my guitar, pretending to read the sheet music. Not bad for a ten-year-old kid, right? Unfortunately, the teacher wasn't impressed. He caught on to my game and told my father, "Stop wasting your money on lessons for that kid."

Unlike me, my brother was an accomplished guitarist who had his own band. I admired him since he was being paid to play rock and roll. Thankfully, he was able to teach me the basics and initiate my teenage music career. As the lead vocalist and lead guitarist, I formed a band called "The Revel Tones" with Chris on rhythm guitar and Joey on drums. Our fourth band member was imported from Avenue T and East 2nd Street. Cousin Vinny would become our keyboard player and second lead vocalist. Vinny, my parents' godson, felt like an actual cousin since he attended many family functions and often vacationed with us. All my friends always called him "Cousin Vinny." He beat out Joe Pesci for that official designation many years before the movie came out.

Our group usually practiced once a week in one of our homes. Sometimes we practiced in my backyard where we would draw small crowds of kids from both East 3rd and East 4th Streets. My brother would make suggestions of songs he thought we could easily master. Usually, they would encompass three basic chord progressions: C, F or G or G, C and D. We also tried to replicate songs we had in our vinyl record collection.

Even with my brother's assistance and record collection, we built up a very limited music catalog over time. We played about twenty-five songs; most were instrumentals that The Ventures had performed. Though we did perform a few vocals, our song list was not enough to make us a complete band. Two of our best vocals were, "Good Lovin" as performed by the Rascals and "Boys," as performed by the Beatles. I still maintain copies of our rendition of these songs that I recorded on my reel-to-reel tape recorder. I consider them to be classics.

Our lack of a complete music catalog really didn't matter to us. We were only fourteen- and fifteen-year-old kids playing rock-and-roll music and having some fun. Then a dose of reality set in one day when we were practicing in my backyard. Just beyond my fence, Donna, who lived on East 3rd Street, started screaming, "Can you guys play 'Happy Together'? Please play 'Happy Together'!" That song was the Turtles biggest hit, which reached number one on the Billboard Hot 100 in 1967. Although we could have mastered the chords to that song, we did not have that record or sheet music for the words. We simply completed our day of practice with our rendition of "Pipeline" by the Chantays. That encounter with Donna made us realize how limited we were as musicians. We considered expanding our musical repertoire but concluded that it wasn't necessary as we would only be playing for our own musical enjoyment.

During a practice session at Chris's house, his father came to the basement to observe. He typically offered obscure criticisms about our music and playing, suggesting he wasn't impressed. However, on this particular occasion, he presented us with an intriguing possibility: his cousin might be interested in hiring us for his wedding. Wedding bands were expensive, and there were few wedding DJs available at that time. Thrilled for the opportunity to earn twenty-five dollars apiece, we eagerly accepted his offer. Unfortunately, no one informed us that we needed to learn the cha-cha, rumba, samba, waltz, or even the tarantella or hokey pokey. We went into this event totally blindsided and unprepared. After our first set, we got a ton of song requests we weren't familiar with. It felt like we were being asked to learn a whole new musical catalog on the fly. With no other options, we played our musical repertoire and finished with "Wipe Out" before we left the building as Elvis would have done. I was so angry with our quasi manager (Chris's dad) for not having better prepared us for our first public appearance. Our teenage musical careers pretty much ended that night. We were all completely embarrassed by that experience. We decided to break up the band shortly after that gig. There would be no encore performances or Oldies Revival Shows for the Revel Tones. I did, however, take a real liking to the Turtles and 1960s music. My wife and I would often attend their "Happy Together Tour" whenever the group was in our area.

Every time we would see the Turtles perform, their show would end with the song "Happy Together." And as the group played it, I could visualize Donna screaming over my fence in Brooklyn, "Can you guys play 'Happy Together'? Please play 'Happy Together'!"

CHAPTER SEVENTEEN

The New Neighborhood

Like Boro Park, the Gravesend section of Brooklyn had its own unique places of business for kids to patronize. Before I could drive or take my bike on long trips, my Gravesend world essentially ran along Kings Highway between McDonald Avenue and Ocean Parkway. There one would find a barber shop, two delicatessens, a bagel store, an ice cream store, a luncheonette, a Chinese restaurant, a hardware store, a pizza parlor, clothing and candy stores, a variety store, and a bank. Of all the establishments, I remember these the most clearly. Since many readers may appreciate my fascination with sweets, I'll begin with my sweet-tasting memories.

The Carvel Ice Cream Store was on Kings Highway between East 3rd and East 4th Streets. It was a huge standalone building with its own parking lot. Under direct orders from my mother, before returning home from school, I was to purchase a Thick Shake or Malted every day from Carvel. My mother wanted to fatten up her twelve-year-old, seventy-five-pound son. While I couldn't drink her milk shakes or egg creams since she had prepared them with raw eggs, she suggested a daily thick shake from Carvel. Out of desperation, she came up with this after-school nutritional routine. How refreshing those shakes were without that raw egg yolk slowly sliding down the back of my throat.

Sometimes I would deviate and get a banana split or an ice cream sundae. My gross tonnage was increasing by the day.

Nat's luncheonette was located on Kings Highway and East

3rd Street diagonally across from the Carvel. We usually made a daily pilgrimage there to buy our packs of baseball cards. The cards always came with a hard stick of gum. We would flip our cards along the East 3rd Street side of Nat's building. Flipping baseball cards at that location became a tradition for the kids in the neighborhood.

Standing, the first player would flip his card by holding it in the middle with his thumb and middle fingers. Cascading to the ground, the card would land either on its face or back. Then the second player, trying to match what the first had done, would flip his card. If the cards matched, the second player won and picked up both cards. If the cards didn't match, the first player would be considered the winner. To be fair, we would take turns being first or second.

Another baseball card game we played on the side of Nat's luncheonette was tossing the cards to see who could get them closest to the wall. This game accommodated multiple players. The player whose card got closest to the wall would win all the cards tossed during that round. There would be some heated arguments on the really close calls, but we resolved the issue by calling for a draw or declining the victory.

Sometimes we played with duplicate cards or with cards of baseball players we didn't mind losing. The stakes mounted when players used newly purchased cards, which may have included some All Stars. All of a sudden, the card flipping and tossing game became more challenging and interesting. Worn out or undesired players' cards would be repurposed for use on one's bicycle. Attached to your bike frame with clothespins, the cards were positioned between the spokes of the wheel to create a loud, motorized sound everyone could hear as we traveled around the neighborhood.

Since Nat's also had a wide variety of candy bars at his luncheonette, the baseball card bubble gum was not the only packaged sweets at his location. There was also the typical assortment of sweet beverages like an egg cream, lime rickey, or a coke, available at the counter. A customer wouldn't usually order a malted or shake there with Carvel being right across the street. Sometimes we would occasionally have breakfast or lunch at Nat's when we wanted to feel like adults or when our parents wanted us out of the house.

H. Adler's Candy Store was located directly across the street from the Brooklyn Savings Bank on Kings Highway just off McDonald Avenue. My friend Richie's parents owned the candy store. Although they had the same candy assortment as Nat's luncheonette, they had something at their location that Nat's could never offer. They had their entire Adler family working there.

In the store were Harry and Henrietta, who were Richie's parents, and his brother and sister, Billy and Rochelle (Shelly). Harry was a very low-key and polite man. Unfortunately, we barely got to know him since he passed at a young age. His family now ran the candy store. Richie had the same demeanor as his father. Always willing to talk about our next outdoor sports activity or the latest magazines or comics that just came into the store, he was also a low-key and unassuming kid. The real quirky characters in that candy store were Henrietta, Billy, and Shelly.

Henrietta was formerly in the U.S. Army. I believe she attained the level of sergeant before her term of service ended. As many of us could attest, she probably could have been a drill sergeant. She would bark orders and scream at us, unlike any other shop owner on Kings Highway. My guess is our treatment stemmed from us being good friends with her son Richie. Maybe she considered us her extended family. Whatever her thought process, down deep, Henrietta really had a good heart and sense of humor to put up with us knuckleheads day and night. She even invited a few of Richie's friends on a camping trip at a place they had rented in Wurtsboro, New York. Imagine her wanting to spend time with us crazy kids on her vacation.

    Billy, the oldest son, also had a good sense of humor. He loved trading putdown barbs with all Richie's friends. Older, he had an arsenal of one-liners. He would have given Don Rickles a run for his money. Billy also was taken from our lives too soon.

    Shelly, the only daughter, was cut from the same cloth as her mother. There were many similarities; speech cadence and sheer volume of her voice are two I remember succinctly. Since Shelly did not have any military experience, I assume her demeanor and aggressive personality came from Henrietta having been her role model. Getting under Shelly's skin and trading barbs with her was a lot of fun. Neighborhood children didn't really go to Adler's for the sweet things or the soda fountain service offered. Although that was readily available, we went there for the friendships developed, the lively banter, laughter, and abuse we would give and receive, every time we sat at the soda counter.

    Directly across from the Carvel, the bagel store was located on Kings Highway between East 3rd and East 4th Street. Many of my friends at one time or another worked at that bagel store. I would eventually join them as I became friendly with the night manager Paulie, a neighbor of one of the owners. Paulie was a jovial, large man in his forties at the time. He reminded me of Jackie Gleason on steroids. Paulie was supposed to be the only night-shift worker, but because of his girth and lack of enthusiasm, he farmed out his assignment to the teenagers in the neighborhood. For a couple of bucks an hour and all the bagels, milk, butter, eggs, and cream cheese one could bring home, you too could become an unofficial member of Paulie's night crew.

    We would retrieve trays of uncooked bagels from the walk-in refrigerator in the back of the store, place them into a large kettle of boiling water, scoop them out, and place the bagels onto an aluminum rack, which had cold water streaming onto them. After first preparing the plain bagels, we would season subsequent batches with onion, salt, sesame, or poppy seeds. The bagels would be placed onto wooden slats made of cedar, which were covered with a hard burlap type material. The bagels eventually made their way into the 515-degree rotating, shelved oven. Using a thick oven mitt, the slats would be flipped after one rotation, so the bagels cooked evenly. On the final rotation, the bagels would be removed using a large pizza-style paddle to be placed into their proper bins. In hindsight, this was definitely a job for an adult. I guess Paulie was unaware of any child labor laws he had been violating at the time. I'm also pretty sure that the store owners were unaware of Paulie's teenage employment service. Working in front of those hot ovens five nights a week was probably negating my mother's after-school weight-gaining program at Carvel.

The bagel store owners had a small truck that delivered bagels throughout Brooklyn. One time I decided to take Daisy for a walk down East 4th Street toward Kings Highway. As we reached the end of the block, their truck, making a loud gunshot-like sound, backfired. Daisy got spooked and slipped out of her collar.

Heading directly into the traffic on Kings Highway, she then ran forward with incredible speed. The traffic light happened to be in her favor, and she somehow ran under the bagel truck that was in a still position at the light. As I began to panic because I knew I could never catch her with her speed, I realized I was near the apartment where my friend Ronny lived. Ronny, a superior athlete with great speed, was nicknamed "The Birdman" because he could fly like a bird. I rang his doorbell and within seconds he was in hot pursuit of my little pup, who was on her way to Avenue S. He miraculously captured Daisy and placed her into my waiting arms. This escape had been Daisy's second near-death experience. Though others would follow, none would be as heart-stopping as the first two.

Two competing businesses I recall on Kings Highway were our local delicatessens. They were Joe's Deli off East 4th Street and Lou's Deli across the street between East 2nd and 3rd Streets. My friends seemed divided about which deli was better. From a proximity perspective, since we lived a little closer to Joe's Deli, we probably spent more time there, while from a hospitality standpoint, Lou's was much more welcoming and had a warmer dining atmosphere. Joe, unlike the more agreeable Lou, had a short temper when dealing with kids like me. Because I preferred Lou's Deli and thought his hot dogs and knishes were superior, I didn't mind going out of my way to eat there.

The last store I will reminisce about is Sol's Hardware store, which was located on Kings Highway between East 2nd and East 3rd Street. The owner, Sol, was an elderly gentleman who pretty much ran his small store by himself with occasional help from his children. Few would think a twelve- or thirteen-year-old would spend a lot of time in a hardware store, but I found myself at Sol's quite often. I can honestly tell you that I can't remember one item I ever purchased there. Did I go because my mother or father needed something? Maybe. Did I go because I needed something for a home or school project? Likely.

Whatever the reason, I mention this experience because I truly enjoyed my discussions with Sol every time I visited his store. He wasn't very busy and seemed to like my company. He would ask about my project, make suggestions, and just liked talking to me. Sol was a religious Jewish man who dressed like many of the people I encountered in Boro Park. I never told him about my part-time job as a Shabbos goy on 58th Street, and maybe me being that type of kid resonated with him in some way. I always enjoyed our visits and was deeply saddened when his son told me about his dad's sudden passing. He was a real mensch!

Kings Highway was the main drag where I spent most of my time living in Gravesend. However, based on need, I did venture to other avenues in the neighborhood. I had a small savings account at a local bank on Avenue P between East 2nd and East 3rd Streets.

A block from my home on Quentin Road, the Chase Manhattan Bank eventually took over this bank. I had no personal relationship with any of the employees of that bank. The building itself was nondescript. The bank products and services were the same as one would find at any bank in the neighborhood. So why would I bother to bring up this establishment?

One day in August 1972, I was in my home when suddenly I heard a squadron of helicopters flying overhead. Police cars with their sirens blaring were driving up and down the streets. What the hell was happening? I stepped outside and noticed the police response was heading toward Avenue P. I immediately ran down East 3rd Street to see what was going on. When I got to the corner, there were police barricades in front of my bank. I later found out that there had been a botched robbery attempt with hostages taken. The perpetrators mistakenly entered the bank after an armored truck had taken most of the money out of it. The big haul they anticipated left the bank with that truck.

Instead, they decided to take hostages in an attempt to negotiate with the authorities for a bigger payday. The robbers held seven bank employees hostage for fourteen hours. As the standoff continued throughout the night, the police created a much larger barrier along Avenue P, extending several blocks beyond the bank location. Police snipers were situated on several roof tops within shooting distance of the bank's entrance.

The people in the neighborhood in typical Brooklyn fashion created a party-like atmosphere where they were allowed to congregate. There was music being played and food on the street as if the neighborhood were enjoying a block party. Only Brooklynites could turn such a serious situation into a celebration. Eventually the unharmed hostages were freed. Things didn't go well for the bank robbers. Does this story seem familiar? The movie *Dog Day Afternoon* was based on this true crime story. When I went to see the movie starring Al Pacino in 1975, I was fascinated by how the film recreated the events that I had witnessed firsthand on just another day in Brooklyn.

CHAPTER EIGHTEEN

PS 215

I lost a full year of school because of all my sixth-grade troubles at Catholic school coinciding with our move to the Gravesend section of Brooklyn. My new sixth-grade experience would be made up at PS 215 in Gravesend. The school was on Avenue S between East 2nd and 3rd Streets. The school principal at the time was Mr. Morris H. Weiss. On my first day of school, my parents brought me to Mr. Weiss's office. He was a very distinguished-looking middle-aged man impeccably dressed in a dark business suit with a white carnation in his lapel. Since he wasn't wearing any religious garb at our meeting, my initial fears were greatly alleviated. He looked like a real cool dude, and he turned out to be one.

My parents went over all the trials and tribulations of my past and the need for a smooth transition to public school. Just like my old principal, Mr. Weiss listened attentively, but unlike her, he acted accordingly. Mr. Weiss came up with a strategy that he felt would make my transition to the public school system an easy one. He placed me in a small class with ten students from different grades. The class was taught by Mrs. Coltman, a lovely middle-aged woman well versed in dealing with children who had emotional and physical shortcomings. There were children who wore hearing aids, had broken limbs, and a hodgepodge of other issues.

I guess Mr. Weiss categorized me as having PTSD from my Catholic school trauma of incoming erasers. It probably wasn't called PTSD back in 1965, but you get where I'm going with this. His strategy was to place me in a smaller class, strictly for educational purposes, and with a regular sixth-grade class for all other activities. I was assigned to Mr. Kerper's class primarily for an easier integration into the sixth-grade mainstream. Mr. Kerper was an okay guy, but I never developed a strong bond with him because of the strange circumstances we were under. That being said, Mr. Weiss's plan couldn't have worked out any better for me. Since I was already well versed with the sixth-grade curriculum, Mrs. Coltman would let me complete my assignments independently, with little supervision. Mr. Kerper's assignment was to help me assimilate with the other sixth graders at the school. Treating me like one of his students, he came through in full measure, while I participated in outside activities only.

Many years later, I was fortunate enough to catch up with Mr. Kerper and Mr. Foti (a fourth-grade teacher) at a PS 215 reunion organized by Brandon Steiner, who wrote the Foreword to this book. I'd say that Brandon is probably one of the most successful and high-profile individuals to come from our Gravesend neighborhood. He is a keynote speaker, author, CEO of the Steiner Agency, and founder of CollectibleXchange. He organized several PS 215 reunions over the years. Thankfully, he invited me to this reunion where both grammar schoolteachers were in attendance.

I hadn't seen either teacher in almost fifty years. To my amazement, Mr. Kerper said to me, "I remember you. You lived on Quentin Road, right?" Geez, only seeing this guy for a few softball games and on Field Day, and he had recalled where I lived. I found this to be totally incredible some fifty years later. Seeing a number of old friends and some sports celebrities at that reunion was fun, but nothing was better than seeing Mr. Kerper and Mr. Foti. I will never forget that day as long as I live. I can't thank Brandon enough for inviting me to this event.

One last word on Mr. Weiss is the debt of gratitude I owe him for having devised that wonderful, personalized game plan. Whenever our beloved principal saw me in the hallway, he would give me a hug, put his arm around me, and ask, "How ya doin' kid. Is everything okay?" He was truly a compassionate soul. I'm sure he displayed this beautiful trait numerous times during his eighteen-year tenure at the school. In fact, I'm convinced that he did because on December 9, 1971, almost two years after his passing, the school was renamed the Morris H. Weiss Elementary School.

On sick leave in 1968, he wrote a farewell letter to his teachers. A quote from that letter read, "I leave my kids. I leave them to you without any worry. I know that you will think of them and work with them, plan for them, and do your best to help them develop the best that's in them, as you would want others to do for your own. They are your immortality as I hope they'll be mine."

Mr. Weiss will always be fondly remembered by all who had the pleasure of attending PS 215, while he was their principal. He was another mensch! (I just can't shake my Boro Park vocabulary.)

CHAPTER NINETEEN
After-School Activities

Like many public schools in the New York City school system, PS 215 offered after-school and summer recreational programs. These programs and activities were designed to keep us kids off the city streets, promote physical fitness, and further develop our personal well-being.

During the school year, we went to PS 215 in the evenings every Monday, Wednesday, and Friday from 7 p.m. to 9 p.m. The program was called "The Night Center." It was managed and coordinated by New York City school teachers. The teacher in charge of our local program was Mr. Flanzbaum. His assistants included Mr. Fisher, Mr. Auerbach, and Mr. Gershon.

We would play basketball, field hockey, Wiffle ball, Ping-Pong, chess, billiards, bumper pool, and other indoor activities. In addition to having time for free play, we had organized league play for many of the sports and tabletop activities. To make the kids feel empowered the staff created a council administered by Mr. Fischer. We would meet regularly with selected team representatives to discuss and resolve members' concerns and issues. A typical issue might be a shortage of free play time or too many scheduled competitions in unwanted athletic events. The council was a collaborative effort that made us kids feel as if we were decision-making adults.

The staff created an annual contest called "Citizen of the Year." Each season, members would accumulate points based on attendance, event participation, committee memberships, individual and team accomplishments, and volunteerism for the publication of our weekly newspaper. We all strived to be the Citizen of the Year!

Our weekly Night Center newspaper was called *The Nite Owl*. The paper would feature team standings and individual statistics for each organized sport we participated in. Our paper would also contain articles written by members to report game recaps and make editorial comments. Ours was all the Night Center's news that was fit to print. I was so proud to see the edition that had Richie's and my name in bold letters as the Wiffle Ball Champions of the year! We used a mimeograph machine to produce copies of *The Night Owl* for distribution. Multiple prints were produced by using a hand crank and forcing ink through a stencil, onto eight-by-fourteen-inch paper. The smell of the ink had an addictive quality to it. For some reason, I loved cranking out copies of *The Nite Owl* just to smell the finished product that came out of the machine. Anticipation of seeing one's printed article offered great pleasure and satisfaction.

When the Night Center would close its doors at 9 p.m., we would head over to H. Adler's Candy Store to revel in our victories or drown our sorrows over a lime rickey or egg cream. On every occasion, you could count on Henrietta telling us it was time to go home and go to bed. It became another neighborhood tradition.

After the school year ended, the Night Center would shut its doors, and a similar outside program would be rolled out during the daytime summer months. One major difference between the two programs was that we took road trips to other public schools within walking distance of PS 215 to compete in softball games. For my very first road traveling team experience, I offer a special shout out to Mr. Diamond. He was one of the nicest guys you could ever meet who took us on many of those road trips.

We were lucky to have him as one of our summer counselors at PS 215.

Both programs provided physical fitness, character building, enhanced skills in writing and social behavior, and created life-long friendships. All of these experiences would not have been realized had the programs not been offered by the City of New York. Having come from Boro Park, I had no idea my world, extending way beyond my block, would be so far reaching. I felt very fortunate being a kid from Brooklyn during this amazing and wonderful time.

CHAPTER TWENTY

The Schoolyard

The unofficial hangout for all the neighborhood kids was the PS 215 schoolyard. Every day after coming home from school, we'd change our clothes, grab a snack, do our homework, and then head back to the schoolyard to play until dinnertime. There one could find anywhere from five to thirty kids playing outdoor games. There were stickball courts along one side of the building.

Unlike the stickball we played on 58th Street, this game included two or four players. We had a pitcher who would throw his Spaldeen fast and on the fly as he aimed at a painted batter's box on the school wall, which represented the strike zone. As in regulation baseball, there were four balls and three strikes per batter and with three outs per team. The batter would get a home run by clearing the outfield fence. Doubles would be hits off the fence, while singles were determined by the batter's getting the ball past the pitcher. The pitcher or his outfielder could catch fly outs.

We sometimes had four games going on simultaneously on the inside corner of the schoolyard. The play got so competitive and organized, we formed our very own stickball league. Stats were kept and a champion was declared at the end of the stickball season.

On the perimeter of the schoolyard were several basketball courts where three-on-three games would be played. Also, in the opposite corner of the stick ball courts, one might find a softball game being played with nine to ten kids on each team. These games usually occurred when there were no stickball or basketball games being played. Adjacent to the schoolyard was a large, enclosed tree-lined grass field, which became known as Mr. Foti's Garden. Mr. Foti was a fourth-grade teacher at the school, who, with his students, grew vegetables during the spring season. In the fall and winter, that garden would become our touch football field. We would have to climb over a gated fence, which had a locked entrance, to gain access to his garden.

This seasonal vegetable garden had never been sanctioned for our personal use as a football field. Although the school administration had heard rumblings of us having used the field to play football, no one prevented us from taking advantage of that soft playing surface. We city kids spent most of our playing time in the concrete jungle. This playing surface, a nice diversion, was certainly much easier on our knees.

Can you imagine all these sports activities going on at one location just beyond the school walls? Our schoolyard became the centralized place where we would gather to play sports and have fun daily throughout the year. I doubt such a phenomenon exists today.

Although our initial intent was to just play sports and have a good time, we developed other skills and learned unexpected benefits that accompanied our sports activity at the schoolyard. Every day, our debating and negotiating skills would be sharpened and put to the test in the schoolyard. Getting a consensus on what sport the group would play sometimes required some serious negotiations. Playing softball required navigating shared spaces; stickball or basketball games already in progress might necessitate convincing participants to switch games or risk accidental injury due to overcrowding. Even the length of a particular game might have to be negotiated. Some of these negotiations could become very heated and argumentative, but most of the time, cooler heads would prevail for the good of the majority. Then the game was on!

Debating skills would sometimes surface while we waited for winners on the sidelines of the basketball or stickball courts. Most of those discussions centered on whose professional sports team or favorite athlete was better. We had to be well versed in team and individual player statistics to have a good chance of winning our argument. There were always the standard arguments: Who was the better center fielder, Willie Mays, Duke Snider, or Mickey Mantle? Or which team had the greatest sports dynasty, the New York Yankees, Boston Celtics, Montreal Canadiens, or the Green Bay Packers? Statistical knowledge was of no use to me since I had been a Mets, Jets, and Knicks fan in those days. Not until the 1969–70 seasons could I proudly gloat and win a schoolyard debate.

One could say there was a rite of passage that existed in that schoolyard. We entered the schoolyard at a young age with undeveloped sports and social skills. Through our association with the older kids there, we developed and honed those skills. We then passed on our knowledge and experience to the younger generation of kids, who followed in our footsteps.

We encountered many mentors in that schoolyard, who shared their sports acumen and life experiences with us. We were very fortunate and grateful to have learned so much from them. I credit my outside bank shot to Howie (also known as H-Factor) for his time and patience with me on the basketball court. I couldn't shoot that shot consistently until he gave me a few pointers. He was the master of the bank shot.

PS 215's schoolyard in Brooklyn was more than just a place to play; it was where lasting friendships began and crucial life lessons were learned. I vividly recall those innocent times and can almost hear the familiar cry of "Who's got next?" echoing by the basketball courts.

CHAPTER TWENTY-ONE

Strat-O-Matic Baseball

When the Night Center closed for the year, and cold weather prevented our playing in the schoolyard, my friends and I gathered in my basement for a season of Strat-O-Matic baseball. I had graduated from Glenn's Challenge the Yankees game to this expanded and more realistic multiplayer and multiteam board game. This tabletop baseball game factored in every individual baseball player's statistics with the intent of replicating his performance for a particular season. Printed player cards with various ratings listed on them and dice were used to play a simulated nine-inning baseball game.

Each year a group of us, usually Joe, Marty, Richie, Dennis, Glenn, and I, would either choose a team or draft individual players for the upcoming baseball season. Then we would put on our managerial hats to compete for that season's World Series championship. Documenting the individual and team statistics as we went along, we usually played an entire baseball season. Making trades throughout the season, we also acted as the team's general manager. One year, I remember Richie having Hank Aaron on his team as his cleanup hitter. I think Hammerin' Hank finished the season with a league leading seventy-five home runs.

Though the player's tabletop performance wasn't always indicative of his actual performance, we were simply having fun playing and enjoying one another's company on cold, winter nights. Being home, I was able to please my parents, since I was off the streets and they could keep an eye on me. Unfortunately, Dad was an early riser because of his overnight shift at the Fulton Fish Market. We would have to play the game with controlled exuberance so as to not disturb his sleep. This was a challenge for us when one of our players did something significant, like hit a home run. On numerous occasions, my mother had to remind us to be quiet. I'm pretty confident she did that at least seventy-five times for Hammerin' Hank. I can visualize it now.

The dice rolled a 2 and an 8 and we shouted, "HOME RUN! HOME RUN!"

My mom then shouted, "PLEASE BE QUIET, DOWN THERE!"

And my dad probably rolled over in bed, totally oblivious to all the commotion.

About ten years ago at the time of this writing, my friend Bernie purchased a Strat-O-Matic baseball game based on the 1971 season. After a round of golf and lunch in Pennsylvania, my foursome of sixty-year-olds played the game at my dining room table for the first time since we had been teenagers. Norm and Steve completed our foursome that day.

These three friends all lived in different parts of the city when they were kids. We didn't know each other until we met at work over thirty years ago. Beyond our shared profession at that time, a fundamental connection existed: our youthful passion for baseball. This shared love led us all to play Strat-O-Matic, and we sought to recapture those childhood moments. That afternoon, we played a single game, filled with laughter and nostalgic recollections of our teenage obsession with it. We made a promise to play again, but it sadly never happened. Perhaps we simply recognized that we were no longer thirteen-year-olds.

CHAPTER TWENTY-TWO

The Ouija Board

Being a kid who didn't want to limit himself to playing strictly sports board games, I purchased a Ouija board for some fun and indoor entertainment. I found the game of Monopoly to be long and boring. I did enjoy being the banker when we did play. Who knew that occupation would be in my future? Certainly not the Ouija board.

I don't remember why I went out and bought the Parker Brothers interactive board game. It may have been from seeing the 1944 movie *The Uninvited,* starring Ray Milland, or maybe it was watching our neighbor Vickie and my mother conjuring up spirits in my kitchen. Whatever the reason, I just knew I wanted to speak to the dead, too.

A Ouija board is a hard flat gameboard with a YES and NO printed in the upper left and right top corners. In the middle of the board are the letters A through M on top with N through Z underneath. Consecutive numbers 1 through 9 with a 0 following the 9 are near the bottom of the board. At the very bottom is the phrase "GOODBYE." The game comes with a small heart-shaped plastic pointer. Near the front of the pointer is a clear, plastic circle the size of a quarter. Two people place the board on their laps facing one another.

They then place their fingertips very lightly on the plastic pointer until it starts to move by itself. We think. Once the pointer is in motion, a player begins to ask questions. The responses could be either numerical, yes or no, or they can be spelled out.

If an answer like a name is requested, the pointer, hovering and stopping over each letter, will spell out the name. When the spirit gets tired, the pointer hovers to the bottom and says GOODBYE. It sounds incredibly stupid, I know. But each participant would swear to the other that the moving pointer seemed independent of the player's direction. We felt like something supernatural was happening across the board once we started.

My friends and I attempted to use a Ouija board, but our session devolved into childish humor, with us using the pointer to make crude jokes and tease each other. To truly experience the Ouija board, I realized I needed someone who genuinely believed in its power. My mother would fulfill this requirement. She seemed completely enthralled with the game, playing with my neighbor Vickie. One night sitting in our kitchen, we asked the Ouija board a million questions. It was very responsive to us. We were having fun until Ouija got a little too creepy and personal with some of the answers to our questions. It told us that our dog Daisy had been reincarnated and in her human form was named Margherita. The response frightened Mom since Daisy translated into Italian is Margherita.

We always thought that Daisy was a highly intelligent dog who had Italian DNA but had no idea she was once in human form. Now Daisy's behavior and innate talent of understanding verbal requests made us wonder if the Ouija board was on to something. I know this is a big stretch, and I don't believe any of it. I doubt Margherita ever chased clothespins on a roof either. However, the answers the Ouija board gave us that night were truly spooky, and my mother was concerned. It didn't help when on that very same evening we had a visitor come into our dining room. And no, the visitor was no Italian family member or friend. The visitor that evening was a very large rat! While my mother and I were watching TV in the living room, I noticed some movement under our dining room table. Daisy was sitting next to my mother on the couch. I got up to take a closer look and made eye contact with this varmint. He quickly scampered down the stairs to our basement.

I asked my mother, "Did you see the size of that thing?"

She responded, "Yes, I did, and tomorrow I am calling an exterminator!"

We went up to our bedrooms and closed the doors behind us. I took little Daisy with me because I didn't want her to be that critter's late-night happy meal. I was right in my assumption that the rat was hungry. During the night, he came back up to our dining room and attempted to gain entry into our pantry.

His gnawing teeth greatly damaged the bottom of the pantry door. He probably would have gained entry had he not been scared off when my dad left for work. The next day, my mother called the exterminator, then packed up my Ouija board and threw it in the garbage pail outside.

For the record, our fat intruder had nothing to do with the Ouija board. The exterminator told us the city was working on a sewer line outside our house. The rat somehow found its way into our house because of all the commotion in the street. He told us it was an isolated incident that sometimes happens when street repairs are being done. My mother didn't hear a word he said. As far as she was concerned, that game brought evil spirits into our home—and it had to go! It was time to say GOODBYE to our Ouija board.

CHAPTER TWENTY-THREE
David A. Boody, JHS 228

After graduating from PS 215, I went to David A. Boody Junior High School, which was located on Avenue S between West 4th and 5th Streets. Thanks to Mr. Weiss and all the great teachers and kids I had met at his school, my transition to this next level was an easy one. I must admit my Catholic school educational background came in handy, too; I felt well equipped to handle junior high. I made the honor roll there even after having cut classes for thirty consecutive days.

I had successfully been intercepting the mailed school notices until a substitute mail carrier foiled my plan with a very late delivery. My all-time consecutive day class-cutting record at Boody JHS came to an end thanks to Mr. Postman. When I attended school, I was an active participant in recreational sports and even became a hall monitor. There were no spanking machines or kids crying in the stairwells at this school. There were some stern and sometimes menacing-looking teachers like Mr. Lippman, Mr. LaManna, and Mr. Tolins. One of them supposedly had a lead pinky finger that would sometimes find a student's noggin, but such behavior was nonthreatening. I never witnessed any bad behavior from any teacher at that school. There were no pointers, metal rulers, or cat o' nine tails being used as weapons at Boody JHS. Also, I never saw a teacher impersonating Sandy Koufax with blackboard erasers. Boody was a completely different learning environment from what I had previously experienced at Catholic school.

I managed to keep out of trouble and made many new friends who came from other elementary schools in the area. One new friend I made was a girl named Adeline, who had come from PS 95. Her friend Carol was dating my friend Jerry. He said Adeline wanted to meet me. We started dating shortly after. In our teen years, such courtship involved hand holding, taking walks, or going to the movies or to the luncheonette for a soda. Despite my having been attracted to Adeline, our relationship was short-lived. One night, Jerry and I were walking the girls back home, taking a shortcut through the PS 95 schoolyard on Van Sicklen Street. Suddenly it began to rain eggs on us by a gang of boys just outside the schoolyard entrance. We all ran as fast as we could. I was a bit faster than Adeline, and unfortunately, she was on the receiving end of a few of those eggs. I went untouched. She felt I should defend her honor and go back and address the gang on the proper etiquette of egg throwing. I, being from Brooklyn, had the street smarts to say, "What are you freaking crazy?" And so, the romance between Adeline and myself came to an abrupt ending that evening.

I would always keep this dating experience in the back of my mind for future reference. Going forward, I would only date girls who could run as fast as me.

That memory wasn't my only experience with egg throwing. One Halloween night, my friends from East 3rd Street and I decided to throw eggs at a city bus. Our target would be a bus that stopped on Kings Highway and East 3rd Street, in front of the Carvel Ice Cream store. Targeting cars, buses, and trains on the elevated line, a commonplace teen activity, required our buying a dozen eggs and waiting for our target while we hid in the bushes near Marc's house. When the bus stopped at the Carvel, we emerged and began hurling our eggs at the bus. It seemed that some of us had stronger throwing arms than we thought and our eggs went flying over our intended target.

Though a harmless ritual on Brooklyn's Halloween nights, this behavior had unintended consequences as our eggs hit unsuspecting victims, including two Dominican nuns as they exited the bus. When the bus drove away, we witnessed the damage we had caused. One of the unintended male victims started racing toward us for retribution. We ran down East 3rd Street toward Quentin Road to escape his clutches. Midway down the block, he realized he couldn't catch us and ended his pursuit. Once again, my running speed came into play with another egg-throwing incident, and, unlike Adeline, my friends managed to keep up with me.

We never expected this outcome when we had decided to throw a few eggs at a city bus. Certainly, our intention had never been to hit or injure anyone, and I never again took part in any such Halloween hijinks.

Besides kids throwing and getting hit by eggs during the Halloween season, one had to deal with other awkward situations during the school year. There were a few bullies who liked to throw their weight around during lunchtime and after the school day. At thirteen years old, I was no Charles Atlas (a famous Italian-American bodybuilder in the 1920s and '30s), and dealing with some of these guys could be really difficult, especially since several of them were older and fresh out of reformatory school. Okay, I'm exaggerating a little, but some of them surely qualified for admittance. I was always one step ahead of them for the most part, but just in case things got out of hand, I needed some insurance.

When friends and I were playing basketball, one of the bigger bullies accidentally took an elbow to his nose, which started bleeding profusely. Nobody was able to assist this thug in his time of need. Now was my chance to be a hero and make a friend for life. Since my mother had always insisted that I never leave the house without a clean, ironed handkerchief, I ran to the boy, gave it to him, told him to tilt his chin upward, pinch the bridge of his nose, and squeeze. I spoke from experience. After his bleeding stopped, our game resumed.

As we returned to class, he thanked me and declared, "Anytime you need my help, just give me a holler and I'll be there for you."

I said, "Great, and by the way, you could keep the handkerchief."

And here began a new and lasting friendship that would remain until the day he dropped out of school one year later. You may have noticed I didn't mention his name in this short anecdote. I'm not taking any chances just in case he learned how to read while he was away in prison.

Remembering my school experiences at Boody, beyond those of Adeline and my bloody-nosed bully, I think of my love for Mr. Kase's shop class. We made such neat things in his class, some that I still have in my possession. My best shop project was a wooden jewelry box that I had made for my mother. She loved her perfectly stained and shellacked jewelry box with drawers crisply lined with a smooth green felt-like material. She proudly displayed her gift on her bedroom dresser. That jewelry box now sits on my worktable in my garage. Instead of rings and bracelets, it now holds nuts and bolts. Mom's probably laughing in heaven that I still have this multiuse wooden box.

A final memory of my school days included going to Gus's Italian deli, which was located on the corner adjacent to the school. Gus's deli offered those who had lined up daily during our lunch period some of the largest, greatest tasting Italian heroes in Brooklyn. A beloved hero sandwich consisted of fresh Italian bread piled high with ham, Genoa salami, Provolone cheese, lettuce, tomatoes, and mustard. Going to that deli was the highlight of my school day.

Even though Gus had nothing to do with our junior high school education, he did teach us one thing. You had to get to Gus's deli early or you would definitely be late for your next class.

CHAPTER TWENTY-FOUR

Abraham Lincoln High School

After graduating from Boody JHS, I was slated to attend Lafayette High School. Your school designation was based on your current home address. I had several friends who were heading to Lafayette, but many more were on their way to Abraham Lincoln High School, where I wanted to go. Since school choice didn't exist in those days, I creatively found a way to be with my buddies. Fortunately, Cousin Vinny lived on Avenue T off East 2nd Street, which was zoned for Lincoln. Just before the new school term, I cleverly moved to Avenue T.

Lincoln High School, located at 2800 Ocean Parkway in Coney Island, Brooklyn, had a very good academic track record at that time. Notable graduates from Lincoln included music legend Neil Diamond and countless professional athletes. Three Nobel laureates in science, who also graduated from Lincoln, were Arthur Kornberg, Paul Berg, and Jerome Karle. All this rich history had absolutely nothing to do with my decision to attend Lincoln. More than likely the proximity to the batting cages, Tilyou Movie Theater, or Nathan's Famous in Coney Island had some bearing on my decision; I was certainly unimpressed by the alumni. My interest in Lincoln's "Rich" history was solely about spending time with my friend Richie, my fellow truant from Boody Junior High.

Richie and I were not the most dedicated or diligent students. We had little to no interest in sitting in a classroom all day. We wanted to go places, do things, and see the world. On the days we felt the need for some fresh air, our adventures would take us all over New York City. With school bus and train passes in hand, we had a free ticket to anywhere, whenever we felt the need to explore. While we sometimes took the El to Manhattan, the NBC Studios at Rockefeller Center was one of our most visited destinations. Many daytime game shows were filmed there before their exodus to California. Attending so often to see shows as *Jeopardy* and *Concentration*, we became familiar with host Art Fleming and announcer Don Pardo on a first-name basis. We even received handwritten answer cards used on the show. Though offered as souvenirs for us to take home, the cards never made their way to Brooklyn. We politely accepted the cards but discarded them before we returned home. It would have been difficult explaining to our parents how we had acquired those parting gifts.

Coney Island was another favorite destination of ours when we played hooky from school. Richie would borrow a roll of dimes from his mother's candy store register. I'm not sure if he ever paid his mother back for those dimes or offered free labor. After a hot dog or chow mein sandwich at Nathan's, we would make our way to the baseball batting cages. There we would swing at hundreds of baseballs from an Iron Mike Pitching Machine that could throw up to 100 mph. We didn't hit many pitches, but it was sure fun trying.

We always wondered why our mothers never noticed the blisters on our hands after a hard day at school. On days when our hands were too sore to hit rubber baseballs, we would go to the Tilyou Movie Theater on Surf Avenue to see a movie that at the time only cost a dollar. That was a great price for high school students on a fixed income of dimes. The aged and dilapidated theater, last cleaned seemingly decades ago, reeked of stale urine and cigarette smoke. Besides us, the only other attendees were a handful of elderly men in lengthy raincoats occupying the rear seats. Fortunately, before the Tilyou's eventual closure in 1968, we had the pleasure of seeing the Beatles' *Yellow Submarine*, a fantastic film for any admirer of the band.

Speaking of movie theaters, I worked as an usher in the Cinema Kings Highway theater during my senior year of high school. This 650-seat theater, formerly known as the Jewel Theater, was located on Kings Highway between East 7th and East 8th Streets. Murray, a schoolyard friend, had told me cashiers, candy and popcorn attendants, and ushers were being hired. I interviewed with the theater manager whose name was Mr. Goldstein. He was a nice man who could have easily been Henny Youngman in another life.

I would meet the requirements of the job if I could arrive at work on time and give the correct change at the candy counter. Mr. Goldstein told me that to attract potential customers cashier positions were only assigned to pretty girls. Once I started working there, I soon got my friends Marty, Joe, and his sister Olga to join the employment ranks. We may all correctly assume what Olga's position was destined to be. She fit the bill as the pretty girl cashier Mr. Goldstein desired. The guys would rotate working behind the candy counter or in the theatre with their trustee flashlights to usher people in the dark.

When we first started working at the theater, the owner would secure old and dated movies, which probably cost a lot less in royalties than first-run pictures. He would also charge considerably less to see a movie at his location. This strategy was unsuccessful in attracting many moviegoers. Most people in the neighborhood were going to see new movies in the larger and much nicer Kingsway Theater, which was located on Kings Highway off Coney Island Avenue. The owner had to pivot with his business strategy and determine a sustainable plan of operation. Of course, this strategy came just months after I started working there.

His new business model was to secure new offbeat movies not easily found in the larger, more established theaters in the neighborhood. His first new movie was a dark comedy-drama entitled *The Boys in the Band*.

The movie, based on an off-Broadway play of the same name, was about a group of gay friends who confronted their feelings and truths at a birthday party in New York. The owner showed this movie night and day for fifty-two consecutive weeks. For this little theater that usually changed movies every month or two, a record must have been set with this film. By the third month, attendance at his showings had dwindled to just a few patrons each time. It was also around this time that I had practically memorized every single line of the film. In fact, my standard response to my mother's daily inquiry about my workday was, "Oh, Mary, don't ask!" a famous quote from the movie I must have heard at least a thousand times. My mother, Maria, adopted the name Mary after immigrating to this country.

Well, this new business model was failing too at the Cinema Kings Highway box office. The owner pivoted once again with something our neighborhood had never seen before. He started importing X-rated movies for everyone's viewing pleasure. The first movie he presented was called *Behind the Green Door*, featuring actress Marilyn Chambers of Ivory Soap fame. When news reached my friends of our movie theater's new business strategy, I suddenly became the most popular guy in the neighborhood. Every friend and acquaintance wanted me to sneak them into the theater via the emergency exit doors. Some of them weren't allowed in the theater because of the age restriction associated with X-rated movies. Did I let those kids in anyway? "Oh, Mary, don't ask!"

Besides being a cashier at the Cinema Kings Highway theater, Olga had other career aspirations. She decided to compete in the Miss American Teenager Pageant held at Palisades Amusement

Park. Rumor claimed that this annual competition, which was held at the park and broadcasted on local television stations throughout the Tri-State Area, was celebrated as the beauty pageant capital of the world. Joe organized our road trip to Bergen County, New Jersey to cheer on Olga for her quest for the title. Several of the PS 215 alum made the long trip to New Jersey, via subway and bus from the Port Authority Terminal. Our early arrival gave us the opportunity to go on almost every ride the amusement park had to offer. After spending an exhausting day there, we settled down for the beauty pageant festivities. The contest started early in the evening. We stayed for the entire show and arrived home near midnight. Unfortunately, Olga didn't win the beauty pageant that evening, but she did retain her title of "Prettiest Cashier" at the Cinema Kings Highway theater.

It is probably clear by now that Richie and I weren't the greatest students. We barely managed to get by. At some point, Richie decided that completing his high school education at Lincoln wasn't going to become a reality. He eventually left school, got his GED (general educational development) diploma, passed a civil service exam, and eventually became a NYC police officer. I, on the other hand, was one course away from graduating from Lincoln.

That course was economics, taught by dear Mr. Schepps, who was a very interesting character. The few times I attended his class, I remembered him discussing his economical view on life. Everything in his world had an economic attachment. For instance, he considered owning a car while living in Brooklyn to be foolish. The few times I met him on the street, he would always be on his bicycle. He could travel to most places using public transport or his bicycle. The school year concluded with my economics teacher assigning me a failing grade of 64. Graduation required a 65, and despite my pleas for that single point, he remained resolute. Perhaps that additional point held no economic benefit for him. Undeterred, I persistently requested that one point daily.

Finally, my pragmatic question broke him: "Do you really want to see my ugly mug around here for another entire school year? Please give me the point, and I'll be out of your life forever." I suppose the prospect of never seeing me again made economic sense, as he finally relented, allowing me to graduate from Lincoln High School. Thank you, Mr. Schepps!

CHAPTER TWENTY-FIVE
Off to Cooperstown

I was the first of my group of friends to get a driver's license. My friend Marty and I took a high school driver's education course so that we, at the age of seventeen, could get our license a year earlier. My dad had already taught me, at sixteen, how to drive. That was the legal age to obtain a learner permit in New York State. One was allowed to take the wheel, during the daytime, if accompanied by a licensed driver and the car was outside the city limits. Since we were often visiting our Long Island relatives, my father allowed me to practice as soon as we crossed the Suffolk County border. This additional practice time convinced my driver's education instructor that I was proficient; he then offered my scheduled practice time to Marty, who had less driving experience.

When I finally got my driver's license, I was eager to use it. My dad would always let me take his car to drive my friends around the neighborhood. We went to hamburger joints like Wetson's near Nellie Bly amusement park off the Belt Parkway. Wetson's was one of the first large hamburger chains to open franchises in the New York market. It was very similar to McDonald's. Their version of the Big Mac was called the Big W. We created a contest to determine who could eat the most Big Ws during one visit.

The unofficial record was six Big Ws. Imagine consuming six of these sandwiches, which included twelve hamburgers, with melted cheese, pickles, and their special sauce on a three-layered bun, all in one sitting. Holy moly!

In addition to going to Wetson's, now that Dad felt more confident in my driving ability, he allowed me to drive to hockey and basketball games in Nassau County and baseball games in Queens.

Since my friends and I, all baseball fanatics, had never been to the Cooperstown Baseball Hall of Fame, I asked my father if I could borrow his car for a day trip. To my complete shock, he agreed, and soon friends, Joe, Marty, Richie, Peter, and I were on our way. Accompanied with both a Hagstrom Map and instructions from my dad, we chartered our course for our 220-mile journey. Despite our great plans, we got lost and arrived to learn that the museum had closed for the day. Using a payphone, I called my father to get permission to stay in Cooperstown overnight. Surprisingly, he agreed and the boys and I, without parental supervision, spent our first night in a motel in nearby Oneonta, New York. We didn't have a change of clothes or even a toothbrush, but who cared? The next day we would witness baseball immortality and get an up-close look at the Babe's bat and mitt.

We got up early, had breakfast, and were the first patrons of the museum as the doors opened. It was a wonderful experience seeing the rich history of our favorite sport. We covered every inch of that museum. We watched vintage films and read every Hall of Fame plaque of our baseball heroes. There were even some artifacts from the 1969 World Champion Miracle Mets on display. After seeing everything that the museum had to offer, exhilarated and joyful, we returned home to Brooklyn. We repeatedly sang a silly song we created about Oneonta for our long drive. When we arrived home on Sunday evening, I was anticipating a lecture from my dad about our poor planning and use of his car. Instead, he expressed interest in the museum and satisfaction that all had gone well.

Perhaps his encouragement of my baseball enthusiasm stemmed from those afternoons spent watching his cherished Brooklyn Dodgers on our black-and-white TV. Or perhaps he was simply pleased to see his son develop into a dependable and trustworthy person, capable of adapting easily and enjoying time with friends responsibly.

CHAPTER TWENTY-SIX

Brooklyn Dudes

Before starting college, a few friends and I decided to take another road trip to Upstate New York. The Brooklyn Dudes on this trip were Joe, Marty, Peter, Dennis, Dean, and Andy. These guys were part of my PS 215 posse. We had seen advertisements in the *New York Daily News* for weekend packages at various dude ranches. One in particular caught our eye because of its proximity to Brooklyn and, more importantly, its price.

The Stanbrooke Dude Ranch in Rhinebeck, New York, a two-and-a-half-hour drive from Brooklyn, offered lodging, food, horseback riding, and entertainment. Some of us had tried our hand at horseback riding at Prospect Park a few times and thought this place would be a little more challenging and fun. It turned out to be more challenging for the wrong reasons. Most of us could handle the riding part since the horses at Stanbrooke were as old and worn out as the ones in Prospect Park. Only Dennis, a first-time rider, was a little nervous about hitching up his horse. However, he was a gamer and up for the challenge.

This dude ranch was not as advertised, at least not on this particular weekend. When we checked in at the front desk, we were informed a plumbing problem had occurred, and, though there wasn't any running water, we were assured the issue would soon be rectified. We proceeded with our check-in. With keys in hand, we were advised to unpack and then visit the stables. Despite a noticeable animal odor in our room, we changed and headed to the stables to meet our horses. The Brooklyn group, with the exception of a clearly uncomfortable Dennis, thoroughly enjoyed the scenic horseback ride. True to his stoic nature, Dennis remained mounted, voiced no complaints, and successfully completed his first equestrian adventure.

When we returned to our rooms, we were hoping to shower and then hit the chow line. That did not come to pass as the water issue remained unresolved. Now smelling like the barn we had just left, us buckaroos headed to the chuck wagon for some grub.

Our dinner was so bad that B-Western film star Gabby Hayes might have passed on it. Our only beverage option for the evening was Mountain Dew soda. We were not very happy cowboys.

As the night progressed and we were having our dessert with some more Mountain Dew, the entertainment coordinator hopped on to the stage. He announced that we would be in for a real treat that evening. He said a famous heavyweight boxer would be performing at the dude ranch that evening.

I envisioned heavyweight champion Joe Frazier and the Knockouts appearing on stage because he was the only boxer with a singing act at that time. Unfortunately, Buster Mathis rather than Smokin' Joe would be showcasing his talents that night.

Buster had been a pretty good fighter in his day and was considered a top heavyweight contender. He had never won any championships, but he did get into the ring with a few champions, including Joe Frazier and Muhammad Ali. Now he was officially retired and is starting a new singing career. How lucky we were to be witnessing history in the making. Tonight's show would be Buster Mathis's debut as a singer and entertainer. Well, Buster should have continued his boxing career for at least another few months. Even better, he should have gone to a trade school to become a licensed plumber. At least we might have gotten to take a shower or had a cup of coffee in the morning.

Buster's Motown interpretations of the Temptations' songs were legendary. His solo performance of "My Girl," where he handled both lead and backup vocals, was a visually demanding feat. Following Buster's act, the entertainment director excitedly ran to the stage, exclaiming multiple times, "Ain't that Buster something? Ain't that Buster something?"

Indeed, Buster was quite something!

Our dude ranch experience, marked by an unappetizing dinner and Buster's ear-splitting performance, concluded with a night at the O.K. Corral. The lack of running water necessitated brushing our teeth with Mountain Dew, which, in the absence of drinking water, we consumed in large quantities. This left us extremely wired and jittery, making sleep elusive without any melatonin or Ambien available at that time.

The next morning, after a breakfast of grits and more Mountain Dew, we yearned for a hot shower and began our drive back to Brooklyn. Throughout the entire journey, we repeated our new tagline, "Ain't that Buster something?"—a constant reminder of our disastrous stay. The return trip to Brooklyn would be silent, a stark contrast to the copious amounts of Mountain Dew that fueled our weekend. In fact, the sheer volume we consumed likely led to a collective aversion; I know I haven't touched the stuff since that ridiculous trip, and I suspect I singlehandedly exhausted my lifetime supply.

When the Brooklyn Dudes weren't riding horses in Prospect Park or Upstate New York, we were looking for fun things to do in our neighborhood. One weekend, we attended a local bazaar at Sts. Simon & Jude church located on Avenue T between West 1st and West 2nd Streets. The group that weekend included Marty, Joe, Richie, Dennis, Peter, and me. We played the carnival games, rode the amusement rides, and ate plenty of sausage-and-pepper heroes along with some zeppoles of course.

At the end of the night, we bought raffle tickets for a chance to win a brand-new Chevy Nova, which was being raffled off the next evening. Marty couldn't attend the following night because of a work commitment. None of us had the winning numbers. As we walked home, we realized we knew Marty's ticket numbers, since our group purchase was in sequential order. We decided to play a practical joke on him by calling his home and telling his parents he had won the new Chevy. Joe volunteered to make the call from a local payphone near the church. He disguised his voice and called himself Father DeLeo. We were hysterical as Father DeLeo congratulated Marty's dad for winning the new car.

Marty's dad was skeptical at first, but when Father DeLeo read off the winning numbers on his ticket, he was convinced he had won the car. We rushed home to meet Marty at his front door as he returned from work. When he arrived, we went upstairs to his apartment to celebrate the supposed new car win, and the family was overjoyed. Marty's dad even planned to pick up his new car the next morning with Father DeLeo. When we finally revealed it was all a joke, they took it surprisingly well, but I left feeling regretful. Sometimes, kids act impulsively without considering the consequences. As well executed as the practical joke was, it was ultimately cruel and something we shouldn't have done.

Coincidentally, Marty's first car ended up being a Chevy Nova, perhaps influenced by our practical joke.

CHAPTER TWENTY-SEVEN

Wildwood Days

Bobby Rydell recorded his hit song "Wildwood Days" in 1963, which was the first time I had ever heard of Wildwood, New Jersey. The lyrics in that song made that beach town sound like such a fun and exciting place to visit on the Jersey Shore. With its sandy beaches, a boardwalk filled with many attractions, thrill rides, and plenty of girls, Wildwood seemed like the perfect destination. Bobby's song mentioned that every day is a holiday, and every night is a Saturday night. We had to see those party lights, wild, wild Wildwood nights for ourselves.

To meet some girls and see the Jersey Shore's version of Coney Island, the guys from PS 215 were interested in another road trip. This time Richie and Dennis drove us on this one-and-a-half-hour excursion. It was going to be a quick trip with a one-night stay in a motel on Atlantic Avenue.

We arrived in Wildwood around lunchtime. The motel parking lot was surrounded by other hotels and motels along the strip. Kids were hanging out on the balconies looking out onto the beaches and streets. Eager to begin our cruising, we were delayed by Richie's car as it lunged forward, struck a concrete divider, and became airborne. The car was teetering on the divider like a seesaw.

As we proceeded to lift the car from the divider, gawking teenagers hooted and hollered at our predicament. We couldn't escape that parking lot fast enough. With a damaged transmission pan, we began our cruising for girls. Unfortunately, the damaged pan created a very loud clanging sound as we were driving. Richie's beautiful 1973 Grand Prix was not going to be the chick magnet we had hoped for. We were getting plenty of attention, but for all the wrong reasons. Unable to continue driving with this loud noise blaring from under the hood, we eventually stopped at a service station. The repair was going to be costly, and Richie asked the mechanic to remove the pan cover to temporarily remedy the situation. He planned on fixing the car himself upon his return back to Brooklyn. He was a pretty handy guy in those days and capable of tackling this repair. Because this incident had taken the better part of our Saturday afternoon, we felt frustrated and took it out on our motel room.

 We didn't meet any girls on this Wildwood trip. I don't recall having gone to the beach or on any amusement park rides either. The only wild, wild thing to have happened in Wildwood was Richie's car teeter tottering on top of that concrete divider. I don't remember hearing those lyrics in Bobby Rydell's song.

CHAPTER TWENTY-EIGHT

Borough of Manhattan Community College

If chowing down on Nathan's Famous Hot Dogs, hitting fastballs off Iron Mike, or getting an occasional correct answer on Jeopardy were qualifiers for entering college, I might have been accepted into Harvard. Since those weren't qualifying events, my only chance of getting into a four-year school would be getting decent grades while in high school. Based on my sorry academic performance there, I didn't even qualify for a good two-year community college. Only one school of higher learning gave this knucklehead a chance at redemption. The only city college of New York to accept my application for enrollment was the Borough of Manhattan Community College (BMCC), where a mercy rule must have been in effect.

Seemingly a school for lost causes and underachievers, BMCC operated without a campus. Instead, classrooms were scattered throughout various office buildings in Midtown Manhattan. Traveling from Brooklyn to Manhattan, I again found myself riding on the F train, but instead of visiting Don Pardo, I was attending college in Midtown office buildings. BMCC seemed like a welcoming place for the lost souls who hadn't yet found themselves. The professors were very nice, and the students were even nicer.

We all identified with one another as having some potential but lacking real direction. I was lucky to make some good friends there. My sidekick for almost every class I attended was my new friend Carlos—a city kid, who happened to have grown up in the wrong borough, Manhattan. I didn't hold his residence or even his Yankees fandom against him. We became quick friends over our love for other New York sports teams like the Knicks. We also shared a crazy sense of humor.

Even after junior high and high school, the urge to skip out of class persisted. Carlos and I would wander around the city in search of entertainment. We visited the Auto Show at the New York Coliseum during its run, strolled through the 42nd Street area of Times Square, absorbing the various scenes (which were abundant in the seventies), and had meals at fancy places like Tad's Steakhouse, where a tough piece of meat resembling shoe leather was offered as a ribeye.

Based on our high school experiences, we shared similar outlooks and, sadly, felt destined for failure. Our future seemed very bleak until one day we approached our sociology professor to express our concerns for our futures. We feared we would lack direction after graduation. Surprisingly, this man quelled all of our silly fears with the following statement: "Are you guys kidding me? I've seen you in action all semester. You have something you can't learn in school. You both have street smarts and common sense. Those two things will go a long way in life. Trust me; you will both go on to have successful careers and lives after you leave here."

A tremendous weight lifted from us immediately. Subsequently, both Carlos and I built successful careers and happy families. Carlos earned his degree from Lehman College and embarked on a career as a schoolteacher. After landing a teaching position in the New York City school system, he fulfilled his career there until retirement. He met Vivian, his future wife, at a bus stop. Their relationship blossomed, leading to marriage and a shared profession as teachers at the same school a few years later. I had the honor of serving as the best man at their wedding. He now enjoys a happy marriage with two children and four grandchildren.

Majoring in economics led to a Bachelor of Arts degree from Brooklyn College for me, where I met Tina, my future wife. Our family grew to include two children and three grandchildren. My forty-one-year career in banking proved the prediction of a community college sociology professor to be accurate. The man should have been a fortune teller.

CHAPTER TWENTY-NINE

The Lottery and the Army National Guard

The one and only lottery I ever won to this point in my life happened on August 5, 1971. On that night, 366 blue plastic capsules containing birthdates for people born in 1952 were placed in a large glass container. The capsules were then, one by one, drawn from the container, to determine draftees for the Armed Services and possible deployment to Vietnam in 1972.

October 1, my birthday, was selected from that glass container on the seventy-first try. The Selective Service System administration would go on to choose another twenty-four plastic capsules to reach their goal of ninety-five for that year's draft. All male individuals whose birthdays were pulled that night were going to receive a welcome notice from Uncle Sam soon. I thought the odds were in my favor since only 26 percent of men born in 1952 were to be drafted. My expectation was not realized since I was with the minority that evening and, indeed, won that lottery. Not too long after that drawing, I received my written orders (which included a subway token) for enlistment in the U.S. Army. I had to report for my physical to Fort Hamilton in Brooklyn.

In September 1971, college deferments for the Vietnam War had largely ended. Even though I had started college before that date, I was now considered eligible for the draft. On September 28, 1971, President Nixon signed into legislation the ending of the Selective Service draft. However, that wouldn't take effect until January 27, 1973. As a result, with college deferments off the table and the president's action coming after Uncle Sam came calling, I was in a real pickle.

I fully expected to fail my Army physical. My allergies to numerous plants were severe, requiring weekly allergy shots for the past six years under medical supervision. Furthermore, I suffered from a deviated septum, breathed through my mouth, and had flat feet. I had resigned myself to the belief that the Army would disqualify me. Clutching my medical records, I reported to Fort Hamilton for the physical. After reviewing my paperwork, the doctor listened to my heart, briefly examined my nose with a flashlight, and declared, "Looks okay to me." Without any discussion of my flat feet, he stamped my papers "Fit to Serve."

Plan A's failure necessitated a Plan B, and as was my custom, I turned to my brother Vinny for guidance and his unique perspective. At the time, Vinny was serving with the NYS Army National Guard at the Marcy Avenue Armory in Brooklyn. His activation during the Great Postal Strike of 1970 had reduced his six-year commitment by a year, meaning his release in 1972 would luckily align with my needs.

With his sergeant and captain's help, Vinny explored the possibility of me succeeding him in his National Guard unit. Fortuitously and with impeccable timing, I was added to the roster—a stroke of luck possibly aided by the U.S. Postal Service Workers. This allowed me to join Company A of the 101st Signal Battalion as a 36 Charlie/36 Kilo, specializing as a pole lineman and tactical wire operations specialist. In essence, I exchanged a potential deployment to the rice paddies of Southeast Asia for working on telephone poles stateside.

During my sixteen weeks at Fort Dix, New Jersey, for basic and MOS training, I encountered physical challenges. While neither my allergies nor deviated septum bothered me, my flat feet and balky knees did. Following eight weeks of basic training, my MOS involved climbing telephone poles thirty feet high for wire missions. Despite the discomfort, scaling poles in New Jersey felt significantly safer than facing combat in Vietnam.

Despite months of preparation for basic training, including running track, weight training, push-ups, and sit-ups as suggested by my brother, I discovered I was not physically ready. My first long march with full gear and weapon exposed this inadequacy. The cold weather, combined with clothing frozen from perspiration and overwhelming fatigue, led to my hospitalization with double pneumonia. Upon recovery, I immediately volunteered to help struggling soldiers who couldn't complete our daily marches.

Leaning on me for support allowed me to walk at a considerably slower pace. This adjustment proved beneficial for both the soldier I assisted and myself.

After finishing basic training and a portion of my MOS training, I was stationed at Fort Gordon in Augusta, Georgia, for the remainder of my six-month active-duty commitment. My previous experience involved climbing thirty-foot telephone poles using gaffs in New Jersey. Now, I was expected to ascend fifty-foot poles in Georgia. Having witnessed fellow soldiers at Fort Dix lose their grip and slide down, some suffering leg injuries and others covered in splinters, I felt the added twenty feet posed an unacceptable risk of physical harm, despite my climbing proficiency.

Observing that some soldiers at Fort Dix avoided climbing due to a fear of heights, I resolved to cultivate a similar fear to change my MOS. Following my refusal to climb the initial fifty-foot pole, and after enduring punishment with KP and latrine duties, I successfully convinced the company psychologist of my fear. He recommended a change of my MOS to company clerk. Consequently, I spent the rest of my active duty with a regular

Army platoon at Fort Gordon, free from pole climbing in both the near and distant future. My remaining time in Georgia and my subsequent National Guard service in Brooklyn would now involve office work.

After completing my six months of active-service duty, I returned home to Brooklyn. For the next six years, I would be required to attend monthly weekend National Guard meetings and a two-week summer camp every year at Army bases located along the East Coast. The Guard enabled me to continue my education and get my four-year degree without a two-year interruption in my studies. I also learned how to maintain a "Deuce and a Half" truck, the nickname for a tactical cargo truck that could carry two and a half tons of materials on and off road. My maintenance contribution was the tedious task of oiling every inch of the exterior of the truck with a solvent.

When preparing for a convoy to Camp Smith near Peekskill, New York, a military installation of the New York Army National Guard in Cortlandt Manor, I, assigned my deuce and a half, prepared it for travel. Having checked the oil, belts, tire pressure, gas level, and side mirrors, I was ready to roll. Positioned last in this particular convoy, I was keeping pace with the other trucks when I suddenly hit a pothole. Apparently, I forgot to fasten the hood clamps to the body of the truck and the hood popped up and blocked my vision. All I could see was army green with a big black star in the middle. With my right-side mirror dangling downward, I decided to gradually get in the right lane, hoping no one would be there. At that same time, the driver in the Chevy Vega directly behind me decided to do the same maneuver. I guess she didn't know the unwritten rule of never passing a truck on its right side.

She ended up hitting my back wheels, going airborne, and being swallowed up in the truck's undercarriage. Dazed rather than injured, she yelled out, "No, no, no, no!" as her dog in an apparent state of shock sat motionless in the back seat. Kinda reminded me of Nipper, the RCA Victor dog.

The convoy ahead saw what had happened and came back to assist us. I was relieved of my driving duties that day and for the rest of my National Guard career. Thinking about what would lie ahead for her, I felt horrible for that poor lady and her dog. Filing an insurance claim with the U.S. government after hitting a military vehicle in the rear while passing it on the right side didn't seem promising.

While serving in the National Guard, I made many great contacts. One of those contacts helped me achieve my first full-time job in banking. At one of our National Guard weekend meetings on Marcy Avenue, I overheard a sergeant who was a marketing director at First National City Bank telling one of my friends about job opportunities at his bank. I wasn't particularly close to this individual, but after their discussion, I asked him if I could apply for a position also. He said, "Of course you can" and gave me the contact information. Using the sergeant as a reference, I then interviewed and, fortunately, was hired in a management-trainee capacity. Sadly, my friend had not advanced during his interview process.

Looking back on that hot August night in 1971, it's clear I hit the jackpot. My time in the National Guard not only let me pursue my education but also steered me clear of Vietnam and paved the way for a career in banking. Considering all of that, it truly felt like winning the lottery.

CHAPTER THIRTY

The New Band

Upon returning home from Fort Gordon several months later, my brother and sister-in-law surprised me with an invitation to join their band. I was taken aback, considering my rusty and limited guitar skills. It had been years since my time with the Revel Tones, and I hadn't picked up a guitar since. However, they weren't looking for another guitarist. Their drummer was moving to Miami within the next year, so they needed me to learn a new instrument instead.

Joey, my friend and bandmate in the Revel Tones, would often leave his drums in my basement between rehearsals, sometimes for weeks. I loved having them there and would spend hours after school playing along to my records on his set. Drumming felt natural to me. Later, after Vinny and Sue married, our Sunday family gatherings in our Brooklyn basement often turned into jam sessions. Vinny played guitar, Sue sang lead—her voice reminded me of Connie Francis—and I was on the drums. My mother especially loved Sue's version of "Mala Femmina." Even now, hearing that song brings back vivid and emotional memories of my parents enjoying Sue's singing in our Brooklyn home.

To gain entry into their band, I would need my own set of drums, take lessons for a year, and study Vinny and Sue's music catalog to learn the necessary drumbeats.

In June 1973 I began my percussion training with drum instructor Dave at the Sid Margolis Guitar & Music Center on Kings Highway and East 18th Street. I outlined my goals, which

THE NEW BAND

needed to be accomplished in the next year. I brought along a list, prepared by my brother, of the different music styles I needed to learn. Dave looked over the list and said if I had some talent and applied myself, we could accomplish my objective. I purchased a used set of drums that were advertised on the music store bulletin board for $150. Vinny and Sue gave me the missing items I would need on a job, which included a travel case, seat, and cymbals. Now all I had to do was learn to play the drums.

In April 1974 I packed my drums for a trip to Vinny and Sue's home in Maspeth, Queens, to meet my new bandmates. I was introduced to Joe who played an electric accordion, and Bennie, the trumpet. They were nice middle-aged men who I felt I already knew because they reminded me of characters from the TV show *Zorro*. This TV action-adventure series was on from 1957 to 1959, and I never missed an episode. Joe reminded me of Sergeant Garcia, who was always trying to capture Zorro (Don Diego's secret identity), and Bennie looked like Don Diego's personal assistant Bernardo. I have no idea why my brain works this way, but just go along with it for this story. We practiced a number of tunes that day with me failing to maintain the drumbeats in many of them. Joe's playing style had a disjointed rhythm.

I was having great difficulty playing along with him. My drum instructor, Dave, suggested focusing on the guitar player to overcome this issue. After a while it seemed to work and I would become a member of the musical group called Just Friends. We would practice together weekly for the remainder of 1974.

Our first performance took place on January 18, 1975, at a Knights of Columbus hall in Queens. I was nervous but managed to play adequately. Sue's stunning vocals, however, unsurprisingly overshadowed Joe and me as we worked to keep time.

That night, I earned $100, plus food and drinks. Later, I joined another band formed by my brother and his talented guitarist friend Charlie. Playing numerous events with both bands provided financial support during my college years. I always played by ear, memorizing the drum parts for our entire musical catalog. And I never revealed Zorro's true identity to Sergeant Garcia!

CHAPTER THIRTY-ONE

Brooklyn College

Having completed my two-year liberal arts degree, I once again sought my brother's advice in picking a major at my new school. Despite having wonderful and supportive parents, their guidance was often broad and not specific to my aspirations. For instance, when I expressed my desire to become a New York State Trooper by taking the civil service exam, my mother's reaction was, "The only uniform you will be wearing is a business suit, white shirt, and dress tie." Similarly, my father offered career advice in the form of a warning: "Whatever you do, just don't become a truck driver." That was the extent of my parents' recommendations about my future career endeavors. Although both comments had their merits and turned out to be correct, I desired a more comprehensive direction at that point in my life.

Vinny suggested a business and finance major in accounting or economics. Given my rather poor command of high school algebra and geometry, I chose to major in economics. It seemed to be the easier route to go, and I thought Mr. Schepps would find it to be a prudent and economical decision. In addition to helping me choose a major, Vinny also recommended that I get a part-time job in sales. He felt a business degree with a sales background would help open some doors for me when I graduated.

After registering and selecting my classes, I then relied on my limited sales experience gained while attending BMCC. I had been a salesclerk at Gimbels Department Store in Herald Square.

Am I dating myself? Yes, Gimbels, not Macy's, gave me my first opportunity to show my sales ability. Gimbels and Macy's were longtime rivals. They opened this store strategically one block south of Macy's in 1910. They were fierce competitors until Gimbels closed that location in 1986.

I interviewed at Gimbels after class one day during the Christmas holiday season. The interviewer had wanted someone with sales experience and was quick to reject me. I asked how one could gain experience without a first opportunity. He seemed to have been taken by surprise with my response and reconsidered. He placed me in the men's clothing department. I was given my own cash register, an old manual style with huge function keys, which I had to prove to the penny every evening at closing. Of course, I had to complete all the change calculations myself. My high school math teachers at Lincoln would have been impressed with my newfound skills.

Most of the time I was folding clothes and putting them back in their proper place. I really didn't have to actively sell anything to anyone. I just directed them to the merchandise they were looking for or told them when an item was out of stock.

With rather limited verbal interaction with customers, I guess my ability to make change and have the correct amount of money in my cash drawer at the end of the night was good for something. At least I could add the name Gimbel Brothers Department Store on my résumé for future employment opportunities.

That seasonal job helped me secure a sales position with Helene Curtis Industries. I would be selling personal-care products like shampoos and deodorants to local pharmacies in Brooklyn, Queens, and Staten Island. In those days, there wasn't a CVS or Walgreens on every corner. There were, instead, many independently owned pharmacies throughout the New York City area. With a wide and vast territory, I found the job challenging since the company had not had a sales force in the metropolitan area for many years. While making my sales calls, I encountered many disgruntled and unsatisfied former customers since the old product line had failed to perform. With unsold and unwanted inventory, store managers, who no longer had sales representatives, turned to me for help. I overcame those hurdles by taking back their unsold products and giving them a credit on our new-and-improved product line. Once again, my Brooklyn "street smarts" came through for me. I became so successful at selling that my employer offered me a company car and permanent position upon graduation. Luckily, I didn't take him up on his offer since independent neighborhood pharmacies would become as extinct as the dinosaur.

I might have reconsidered, however, if my very own cash register had been part of the offer.

Once again, this time with beneficial education and employment advice, Vinny had guided me through some weighty decisions. Where would I have been without him?

With my classes set and a part-time job in place, I realized my social life at school was next on my agenda. Several friends suggested joining a house plan to get fully integrated with the school's social and intramural sports activities. My friend Marty from our schoolyard days had graduated from Kingsborough Community College at the same time I graduated from BMCC. He was also attending Brooklyn College, and we decided to pursue our house plan membership together.

At Brooklyn College, house plans were similar to local fraternities and sororities, operating independently without national affiliations. To find the best fit, we would "rush" multiple house plans, attending their social events to meet members. Our criteria focused on sports and social activities. After just one night of rushing, we were drawn to Battle House. The members were appealing, and they offered a desirable balance of our interests. Battle House had an edge because I knew several members from

Lincoln High, and Marty knew others from Lafayette High. We also felt the most comfortable with the Battle House members we met that evening.

The entry protocol for the house plan involved an intense interrogation by its members. Our experience felt like a wartime interrogation. Imagine being surrounded by twenty to thirty guys in a dimly lit, smoke-filled room, with a harsh sun lamp shining on you. The questioning began with simple requests like, "Tell us a little bit about yourself," but quickly escalated to more difficult scenarios.

I recall one absurd hypothetical question: I was in a sinking rowboat with my mother and girlfriend, and I could only save one. The other would drown. Naturally, there was no right answer to this foolish question, and any response would be deemed wrong. They would then proceed to tear apart my decision, accusing me of causing the death of a loved one. This ridiculous ordeal lasted for nearly an hour. I guess if they couldn't get me to have a nervous breakdown, I would be considered Battle House material. After the interrogation, a vote would be taken, and the majority rule would decide my fate. If we were lucky enough to be selected, the next thing to look forward to would be enduring the hazing and initiation process, which was even more intense nonsense. They did stupid things to you like write obscene things all over your body, using permanent magic markers. I remember taking a Brillo pad into the shower with me to remove all that ink. It was probably the longest shower of my life. I practically took off a layer of skin during the cleaning process. I still might have some written obscenities in the middle of my back that I'm unaware of. In the end, it was all worth it.

I formed strong bonds with many of the guys from my age group that still exist to this day. That bond developed through various activities over time. We would be together in the cafeteria, at classes, playing sports, or at our house plan apartment.

Most house plans rented apartments in the Flatbush neighborhood. They could be in someone's basement or above a retail store. Our apartment was above a storefront on Flatbush Avenue near the Sears Roebuck, not far from the Kings Theater. Our apartment served as the central hub for our gatherings, from meetings and parties to casual hangouts. Friday nights were the designated party nights back then. Throughout the school year, we planned parties at our Battle House apartment, coordinating with girls who had their own house plans. We also occasionally attended their parties when invited.

While refreshments were a rarity at our place, most nights consisted of enjoying each other's company and listening to music from our record collection. "Can't Help Myself" by the Four Tops often played as the girls arrived. It was a pleasant and laidback way to socialize and meet new people. Before our parties began, we typically visited "Slow Joe," the bartender at the neighborhood bar across the street. He'd serve us tequila with a beer chaser—a drink that gave us the courage and energy needed for the night. If the party turned out to be a disappointment, we'd return to the bar to commiserate about our wasted evening. Incidentally, "Slow Joe" earned his moniker due to his remarkably slow pace in preparing drinks.

Representing Battle House in sports was very important to me in college. Earlier, during my senior year of high school, I tried out for the Lincoln High basketball team and made it through the first two rounds of cuts. Ultimately, I didn't make the team. Coach Tayer explained that because I was a senior, and the bench was reserved for developing younger players, he couldn't offer me a spot, especially with his starting lineup already set. He asked why I hadn't tried out for the team before. I explained that a recent growth spurt had increased my confidence in my ability to make the team. Although I was upset about not being selected, I appreciated Coach Tayer taking the time to explain his reasoning, which helped me feel better about myself.

Arriving at Brooklyn College as a junior, I found the basketball team's skill far exceeded my own athletic capabilities, preventing me from joining. Nevertheless, Battle House provided a great chance to play and compete in a structured intramural league with my friends. We participated in organized sports every Monday and Wednesday at midday. We were a competitive group, holding our own in basketball, football, volleyball, soccer, and field hockey. While championships eluded us, we enjoyed our weekly sporting activities, nonetheless.

Our college had a weekly newspaper, *The Calling Card*. It was always a thrill to see our names and sometimes photos published, detailing our game results.

Battle House even had its own team photographer, Mike, who documented every game with photos and 8MM film. Years later, I transferred those films to VHS tapes and gave them to my Battle House friends as a memento. Now on DVD, those old recordings allow us to relive our younger days whenever we get together.

CHAPTER THIRTY-TWO

College Road Trips

During school breaks, beyond local social and sports events, we embarked on road trips. In April 1974, seeking new experiences, we planned a spring break trip to Miami Beach, Florida. Faced with limited funds and unreliable vehicles, we needed a budget-friendly travel solution. We explored using a car transportation service. Harvey took the lead and found a company that transported cars for snowbirds to Florida. He successfully arranged for two cars for our journey South and three for the return home.

The agreement required us to drive the cars without pay, cover gas and tolls, and deliver them to the owners' homes within three days of departure. We also had to take along some of the owners' personal possessions, which included luggage and other items like lamps and small household appliances. With the cars already packed to capacity, we were challenged to find a place for our own luggage. My car included Billy, Richie (the Rube), Marty, and Neal. Harvey rode with Brad, Dino, Barry, and Mike. We couldn't secure a third car going down, so we all chipped in for Stu's and Mark's airfare. John and Howie also flew together on their own. Our spring break destination was the Sun City Motel on Collins Avenue in Miami. This long car ride to Florida had several challenges. My car was a small two-door Ford sedan with no air-conditioning.

I volunteered to drive the first leg of the trip because I liked to drive, and I was a horrible copilot. Once I got behind the wheel, I wouldn't relinquish it. After every pit stop for gas or food, the guys would ask if I was tired yet. I would say no and continue our journey. I drove all the way to the South of the Border attraction located in South Carolina. My goal was Florida or bust, but my friends weren't on board with my plan. Beneath the Pedro's Sombrero Tower landmark, the group insisted on a new driver. I eventually gave in, passing the car keys to Marty for the next part of our journey. However, just moments after he took control, Marty veered off the road and onto the highway shoulder. As the car tilted precariously, we all yelled, "Pull over, Marty!" His driving stint on I-95 was quickly over. Unlike my experience with an Army truck, he successfully changed lanes without cutting off any other vehicles.

Billy took over from Marty, and then the rest of us drove in shifts, reaching our Miami destination in less than twenty-four hours. This left us college guys with twelve hours to cruise for girls along Collins Avenue, while driving Grandpa's car, still full of his belongings.

It's funny, practically every girl we met during our Miami trip that week was a Brooklyn College student. We could have just hung around New York, gone to Brighton or Manhattan Beach, and saved some cash. But what kind of adventure would that have been? Then again, you wouldn't exactly find many college girls on Brooklyn's beaches in chilly April.

Harvey's drive South was also challenging. Despite his newer, air-conditioned car, their speeding pushed the vehicle's limits. Dino was stopped for driving 110 mph on the interstate and had to rouse the sleeping Harvey in the back seat to retrieve the car registration. When Harvey reached for the registration in his pocket, the officer drew his revolver, likely because most drivers keep these documents in their wallets. Of course, the officer's response in this situation was understandable. Though nobody was hurt, they certainly had an interesting story to share when we all arrived at the Sun City Motel.

Upon arriving at the hotel, we split our group into three rooms. Pranks became a regular part of our days. Since we all had long hair, hair dryers were essential items we carried. These became ideal prank tools for launching baby powder attacks. We would position the powder over the hair dryers, creating a large cloud that would engulf anyone entering our room. Our antics closely resembled the gags from the *The Soupy Sales Show,* which aired nationally in 1959.

Our hotel pranks frequently involved shaving cream. One trick was the classic shaving cream-filled paper bag placed outside a door, ready to be stepped on and splattered into the room. Another involved a hidden dollop of shaving cream under someone's pillow, guaranteeing a messy surprise. We once tried this on Richie, placing the shaving cream under his pillow while he and Mark were out. When they returned, Mark unknowingly grabbed the pillow and playfully whacked Richie, covering his face.

Mark's stunned reaction was a moment we wish we'd captured on film. The scene was reminiscent of a Three Stooges routine, just without the cream pies.

Expanding our repertoire, we turned to water for our next prank. As we opened the door for Harvey, we hit him with a bucket of water. Soaking wet, he returned to his room to dry and change clothes. He exited his room wearing a very loud, floral-patterned shirt, which we called his "muumuu" shirt. It looked like something you might see on Hawaiian pop musician Don Ho or an eighty-year-old Floridian resident.

Attracting the attention of some young guys, Harvey was soon surrounded by them. They started verbally taunting him and then it escalated into a physical altercation. Dino banged on our door for help, but we, fearing retribution for Harvey's bucket bath, refused to open it. Dino lost control and to get our attention put his fist through our window. Running down the stairs, we rescued Harvey from his "muumuu" beating. The moral of this story was never let Harvey go clothes shopping alone.

It's a wonder the Sun City Motel didn't charge us extra. Between the shattered windows and broken locks, the disarray of the furniture, the remnants of baby powder and shaving cream, and the absence of towels, one would expect a surcharge. Perhaps the motel manager was cowed by Harvey's muumuu. Then again, maybe he confused Harvey with a resident of nearby Century Village, given their similar fashion choices.

With three days left to get our new rides back to Brooklyn, we decided to take a detour and head to Disney World in Orlando. Disney World opened in October 1971. It was only a few years old when the Boys of Battle House were ready to conquer it. And conquer it we did. We attacked every Disney character who crossed our path, as we attempted to pull off their rubber heads and hands. Having asked the characters to pose for a picture with us, we proceeded to get them in a headlock for our Kodak moment. We posed for pictures with all the princesses and ride attendants who would tolerate us. Throughout the day we also made passes at every unescorted female patron at the park.

As luck would have it, my only legitimate chance of meeting someone on that trip came the day we were leaving Disney. A very pretty girl from Rhode Island found my stupidity amusing. She had just arrived in Florida that day. She wanted to hang out with me and my friends for the week. We couldn't stay, however, because our thirty-six-hour window to return the cars to Brooklyn was rapidly closing. We exchanged home phone numbers and addresses before I left Disney that night. I did receive a nice letter from her shortly after our brief encounter. I wrote her back, but that letter would go on to be the last communication we had. As they say, timing is everything in life. Maybe if we had cell phones in those days and the ability to FaceTime one another, that relationship might have flourished. It's fortunate things worked out as they did. Rhode Island would have been such a schlep. More importantly, I wouldn't have the wonderful family I now have.

On this trip we witnessed one of the most famous moments in baseball history. Sitting all together in a room in Sun City, we saw Henry "Hank" Aaron break Babe Ruth's career home run record, by hitting number 715 on April 8, 1974. We still consider him, rather than Barry Bonds, to be the all-time leading home run champion.

My second adventure with the boys was a canoe trip to "shoot the rapids" in Skinners Falls near Pennsylvania. This group included Battle House members John, Mark, Steve, the Rube, Dino, Brad, Gersh, Stu and his friends from Coney Island (Chicky and Bruce), and my friend Dennis from PS 215. We drove our convoy of beat-up cars from Brooklyn to the Delaware Water Gap in the summer of 1974. We brought along our swimsuits, a change of clothes, and lunch for our day on the water. Some of the guys also brought a lot of beer for the occasion. Our drive there was uneventful except for the many roadside pit stops we had to make, thanks to all that beer.

The discussions in the car centered mostly on the campgrounds, our rented canoes, and possible nightlife we would encounter. We were all extremely excited about our great adventure outdoors. Once we arrived, we changed into our bathing suits and jumped into our rented canoes for our trip down the Delaware River. We all brought our lunch, which we intended to eat at our first rest stop. Our other belongings remained in our vehicles.

The canoe trip started at a point where the waters were calm, and we could enjoy the scenery and surroundings. Within minutes, however, we were swept up in a current, which had speeds for which we were not prepared. Almost every canoe capsized in instant succession. Hanging on to our paper lunch bags, we bounced off sharp rocks in the water like a ball in a pinball machine. By the time we reached calm waters, we had all suffered cuts and bruises from head to toe. Bloodied and beaten, we retrieved our canoes and headed to the rest stop. My ham-and-cheese sandwich was now a soggy soup sandwich.

This water fiasco was just the first sign of worse things to come. We eventually returned to the campsite, changed into dry clothes, and went out to dinner. There was no nightlife to speak of in the area, so after dinner we returned to the campsite and turned in. A pretty girl suddenly appeared out of nowhere and asked us for directions. Separated from her group, she was wandering around the campsite. We gave her the nickname "High Low." I don't recall why we assigned that name to her, but we must have had our reasons. All the guys jumped to attention to assist Ms. Low. Upon finding out her missing companions were a bunch of Hells Angels, we quickly sent her on her way before any additional trouble came calling.

Sleeping in the wilderness didn't agree with most of us kids from Brooklyn. Some of the guys and I decided we might be better off sleeping in our cars.

I had been driving a 1967 yellow Volkswagen Karmann Ghia. This used lemon replaced my beautiful '66 VW Bug, which was stolen in front of my house several months after I had purchased it. That car was in pristine condition and had been well maintained by its previous owner. The VW lemon I was now driving was nothing but trouble from the day I took possession of it. A person couldn't get much of a car for $500 dollars back then. I did expect some trouble when I purchased it, but this car exceeded my expectations.

On this night, my car was not only my means of transportation, but it would serve as my sleeping quarters at this campsite. As I tucked into the cramped back seat, I pushed out the rear window for some fresh air. Unlike many windows, which roll up or down, this one was on a hinge that pushed outward. With my slightest nudge, the window flew off the body and onto the grass. My friends got a chuckle out of this, but I was not amused. Hating this car with a passion, I taped the window to the frame and attempted to go to sleep. With maybe a few hours of shut-eye, I joined my friends for breakfast before we headed back home. One memory of that morning was watching Stu's friends Chickey and Bruce brushing their teeth and using a can of beer to rinse. The scene reminded me of my Mountain Dew weekend at the dude ranch. Water must have been scarce back then. Now the convoy was ready to roll, and we were off to the races to see who would get back to Brooklyn first.

In his haste for a better post position, Stu, jockeying his car, side-swiped the driver's side door on Steve's beautiful blue VW Bug. Everyone but Steve found this to be hilarious. With Dennis as my passenger, my four-speed piece of crap was in the last position of our convoy. Chugging along, we were struggling to keep up with the rest of the boys. After about thirty minutes into the trip, my car suddenly slowed down and couldn't accelerate over 20 miles per hour. Apparently, I had blown two of the four cylinders on those hilly Upstate New York roads.

Driving for at least four hours and at a turtle's pace, we proceeded to Brooklyn without hazard lights. Staying in the right lane, we noticed cars honking and people waving their middle fingers at us. Happy to be out of the Delaware River, close to the ground, and far from Seabiscuit at some dude ranch, Dennis seemed unfazed during our very long ride back to Brooklyn. A ride I will never forget.

CHAPTER THIRTY-THREE

COLLEGE RIDES

During our college years, our transportation options were quite basic, maybe a notch above a horse-drawn buggy. Since most of us couldn't afford decent used cars, we ended up with older vehicles that had accumulated a lot of miles. I personally paid around $500 each for my first two VWs. I stepped up in class with my 1963 Volvo P 1800, which set me back $1,000. This car was by far my coolest ride. I first laid eyes on that model while watching Roger Moore drive it in the TV series called *The Saint*. Imagine me driving the same car as an international vigilante investigator.

Unfortunately, the car was international as well because replacement parts came from every corner of the world. Maintaining that vehicle proved too expensive, forcing its sale after Brad tried to change the water pump at John's residence. John's driveway, specifically its apron, was a rare spot where we could undertake such auto repairs on the streets of Brooklyn. When the scope of the job became too challenging, we would take our foreign-made vehicles to Nunzio off Avenue X and MacDonald Avenue. Nunzio and his brother were good foreign car mechanics. Unfortunately, in those days, repairs done on foreign cars were much more expensive than those on American cars. At that time, I decided to buy my first American car.

I purchased a used 1971 Ford Pinto, and I managed to keep that car on the road until mid-1980. After I had owned the car for a few years, the body began to rust everywhere, and since I couldn't afford the cost of a body shop repair, I did the repairs myself. The floorboard in the car was so severely rusted that every time I drove over a large puddle, the interior would fill with water and saturate me and the interior of the car. I had to keep an extra pair of pants, shoes, and socks in the back seat for emergencies. I replaced the floorboards with aluminum sheets and steel beam supports for the bucket seats. I undercoated the chassis and did the body repair on all the fenders. I sanded down the entire car in preparation for an Earl Scheib $29.95 paint job. I had the red car painted blue to feel as if I had purchased a new car. I did such a great job on that car that my mechanic wanted to farm out his body work repairs to me on the weekends. I had zero interest in having that sideline business. I was just interested in keeping my wheels on the road and my clothes dry.

CHAPTER THIRTY-FOUR

Back at School

With school back in session, I was about to find out if my former sociology professor at BMCC had been correct in his assessment of my capabilities. Would I succeed at my new school? Would I pass my tests, write term papers, get passing grades, and graduate with a degree majoring in economics? Yes, yes, yes, and yes! Just not as you might imagine. I still had a penchant for cutting classes and enjoying my outside activities. Instead of hitting baseballs in Coney Island with Richie, or seeing the sights in Times Square with Carlos, I played cards in the cafeteria and participated in every house plan intramural sport activity available. This time I played hooky with my Battle House buddies.

To get passing grades for the classes I missed, I had several strategies. I would photocopy the notes of the smartest girls in those classes. Those beautifully handwritten notes would be my own personal CliffsNotes to study. From time to time, the guys in the house plan would come across a copy of an upcoming exam. I had no idea how they accomplished this feat and really didn't care. I do know that I got my highest grades when a copy of a test magically appeared on exam day.

When I was challenged with a term paper I didn't want to write, I would buy one from my friend Murray. He had a little side hustle going on at the school. Just for me, he would create an original term paper never to be used again. Murray produced these truly incredible papers with such ease and speed.

Remember, there were no home computers in those days. He was cranking these things out on an electric typewriter. The guy was simply brilliant and a very good typist. He went on to have a successful and long career as a senior banking executive. Without Murray's assistance, I'd still be at Brooklyn College. Once again that BMCC sociology professor was correct in his assessment of my ability to get by and navigate the world.

Hanging out with my house plan buddies in the Boylan Hall cafeteria was something I really looked forward to. Every morning before our first class, we would meet at our assigned table. We would have coffee and sometimes breakfast together. The first conversation of the day involved the length of time it took us to find a nearby metered parking space. The parking meters were for multiple hours at a cost of one dime per hour. The next challenge of the day was to see if the meter would accept the bingo chips we had filed down the night before. This effort was our ingenious way of saving a few shekels every day. Who knew we would become college counterfeiters?

After a spirited discussion, we then needed to decide whether to attend our first class or remain at the table to play cards. We played Spades almost daily, sometimes all day.

Instead of going to Coney Island or Manhattan to visit my old TV friends, now with my Battle House friends I'd be playing Spades. For pocket change, we played each game with a partner. Now you see why we needed those bingo chips for the meters. That table was our central meeting place for all our activities. We would go to classes in groups, eat meals there, play cards, assemble before-and-after intramural sports activities, and schmooze with the girls from other house plans. This place is where I met my future wife, Tina.

I was coming off a broken relationship with another house plan gal I had dated for almost two years. Because Tina had gone on a few dates with two of my friends, I knew her from social events we mutually attended. In fact, at one such event, which was held at Your Father's Mustache in Manhattan, she began hurling popcorn at me while we were both sitting with our dates. Maybe she thought it was some bait to reel in this big fish. Over time, we would gravitate to one another at that lunch table in Boylan Hall. I eventually asked her out on a date, which she accepted under one condition. Rather than go to her house, I had to meet her at school. Though I thought the request was odd, I complied. Later I would find out that Tina's mom would not have approved of our dating. She wanted Tina to date only nice Jewish boys. This view seemed odd to me because at that time I had witnessed many interfaith relationships at school.

In fact, my previous two-year relationship had been with a Jewish girl, and I never felt my religion to have been an obstacle. Tina and I dated for two months and got along splendidly. Unusual for me after such a brief courtship, I even brought her home to meet my parents.

One day, Tina called to end our relationship. She had told her mother about us, and her mother was so angry that she insisted we break up. I was upset, even though I understood her mother's reaction. My own mother wasn't thrilled about us dating, either; she had her heart set on me bringing home a nice Italian girl, preferably a Sicilian.

Tina stood apart; our compatibility was exceptional. We rarely argued over trivial matters and consistently shared perspectives. While marriage wasn't an immediate goal, I believed our relationship held unique promise. Ultimately, however, it wasn't the right time for us. Both dejected, we agreed to stop seeing each other and went our separate ways.

Following a series of disappointing school relationships, I resolved to broaden my horizons beyond Brooklyn College. This didn't involve extensive travel; some friends from Battle House and I began going to clubs in Bay Ridge, Brooklyn, and Nassau

County, Long Island. The Brooklyn disco scene felt artificial and reminiscent of *Saturday Night Fever*. I lacked John Travolta's dance skills and disliked disco music, which only amplified my dissatisfaction.

Long Island, however, would prove to be a different story. The girls we met there were older and seemed more grounded and well balanced. Most of the hookups took place at the bar where dancing wasn't a requirement. I dated several girls with vastly different backgrounds. Many of them were out of school and working full-time jobs. Some were even young, divorced women. This arena was a whole new ballgame for me and my Brooklyn friends.

Though an exciting time in my life, I couldn't get Tina out of my head. I would see her in the hallways at school, and our eyes would connect, and she'd make an immediate turn left or right, to avoid me. After one such encounter, I remember having told my friend Marty that I was going to marry that girl someday. "Tom, you're crazy" was his response. Marty knew a thing or two about Jewish mothers since he had a very dominant one at home.

I wasn't going to give up and devised a plan to get Tina back. We had a mutual friend named Robert who attended our school. She knew him as a classmate, and he was my old friend from PS 215. When we were kids, Robert was known in the schoolyard as "Wabbit" after the Bugs Bunny cartoon character. He was a wisecracking, funny kid who brought out the Elmer Fudd in all of us.

I asked Wabbit to approach Tina and tell her about his family background. Wabbit's mom was Christian, and his dad was Jewish. They were a happily married couple with two well-adjusted kids. I wanted Tina to visualize the possibilities. On several occasions throughout the school year, Wabbit did speak with her on my behalf. Unbeknownst to me, Tina acquiesced to her mother's desires and dated only nice Jewish boys during our year of separation. Rather unhappy, she compared her dates to me. I had no idea I was her gold standard in her dating game. Surprisingly, her mother wasn't overly impressed with Tina's suitors either.

After Tina's unsuccessful attempts to both please her mother while trying to meet someone she liked, she spoke at length with her mother. "I did what you asked and it's not working out for me. Isn't it crazy that everyone I date is being compared to Tom. There's no chemistry or sense of companionship with any of the boys that I've dated. I'm going to call Tom and if he's still interested, I'm going to see him again."

Her mother saw how unhappy Tina had been and finally consented to her reaching out to me. Almost a year to the day of our breakup, Tina called me at home. I had been watching Sunday football with my father and brother when my mother picked up the phone. She said, "Thomas, Tina is on the phone for you." I ran upstairs to my room to pick up the call. She was upset, said she had made a terrible mistake, and wanted to know if I was seeing anyone.

Though dating, I was not committed to any one girl at that time. She asked if I could meet her that afternoon at the El Greco Diner in Sheepshead Bay, a familiar place for us. I was both sorry for her having been so upset and overjoyed that she had reached out to me. You had to know that I was smitten with her, because I would have never gotten off my couch in the middle of a Jets game for anyone. When I reached the diner, we warmly embraced and shared a gentle kiss. After hearing her parents were on board with her decision, we made plans to get together that following weekend.

For the entire week leading up to our date, I envisioned a scene from the 1967 movie *Guess Who's Coming to Dinner*. So psyched, I had been preparing for the worst possible outcome. However, Tina's father, Bert, greeted me warmly at the front door. I was introduced to Tina's sister, Nadine, and her brother-in-law, Marty. They had just finished a champagne toast to Marty for his acceptance into law school. I was offered a glass and joined the celebration. Tina finally arrived coming down the stairs like Loretta Young would have done on her old TV show, *The Loretta Young Show*. However, she was not in formal wear, but in jeans like most nineteen-year-olds at that time.

We left on our date without my meeting Tina's mom, Annabelle. When I asked Tina about her whereabouts, she told me her mom was dealing with a migraine. I was hoping that I wasn't the cause of her neurological illness.

I was relieved to discover that Tina's mom suffered from migraines long before I came into the picture. I already had a track record of giving people headaches, and I didn't want to add another person to my list. That warm greeting and champagne toast with her family was a sign of acceptance and better days ahead. Many thanks to my friend Wabbit and to all the nice Jewish boys who dated Tina during our yearlong hiatus.

CHAPTER THIRTY-FIVE
Transcendental Meditation (TM)

Sometime in 1974 the college, dating, and part-time employment experiences started creating some tension and anxiety in my life. With a need for assistance in dealing with my stress, I could easily have turned to the drug scene, which many of my contemporaries chose; instead, I sought a natural and holistic approach through Transcendental Meditation (or TM as it was referred to back then) offered as an off-campus course. Developed by Maharishi Mahesh Yogi, his certified instructors were teaching the technique in a home on Bedford Avenue, near Brooklyn College.

I had first heard about TM listening to radio shock jock Howard Stern. He was a strong proponent of TM, exalting the positive effects it had on his life. Many other famous celebrities and athletes were also vocal supporters of this form of meditation. The individuals who got my attention at that time were the Beatles, Jets quarterback Joe Namath, Philadelphia Phillies shortstop Larry Bowa, Portland Trail Blazer Bill Walton, and movie star Clint Eastwood, to name a few. All would mention the many health benefits of TM. The American Heart Association said that TM could be considered as a treatment for hypertension.

Now fully engaged and excited about the possibilities, I mentioned my intentions to some of my house plan buddies. Only one friend, named Big Mike, thought it might be a good idea to join me on this self-help endeavor. After attending group meetings and one-on-one sessions for weeks, Big Mike and I completed the course and felt well on our way to peace and tranquility.

The practice of TM involves the silent repetition of a mantra, which is specifically chosen for each individual. I was instructed to keep my mantra confidential, as disclosing it could potentially interfere with my concentration during meditation. By silently repeating the mantra for approximately twenty minutes twice a day, I experienced positive outcomes.

We practiced independently and noticed some benefits, though I seemed to have been more deeply involved than Big Mike. During a meditation in my bedroom, I once became so relaxed that, when the telephone rang, my entire body began to tremble from the ringing sound. Big Mike didn't experience the same benefits as I did and eventually gave up on TM. I continued meditating until I graduated college. I stopped meditating regularly once I started working full time. Even then, one wouldn't close his eyes for twenty minutes commuting on the F train. Working two jobs, I couldn't incorporate meditation into my schedule at home because of the long hours I was keeping. I did, however, get into a routine once I moved to Long Island and traveled in the safer environment of the Long Island Railroad.

Because of my longer work schedule, even that effort eventually lessened as I kept falling asleep on the train. Nonetheless, I became fully engaged again with Transcendental Meditation a year after I retired. There were several reasons for that year's delay. First, I wanted to undergo all the orthopedic surgeries I had delayed while employed. With two knee replacements and one hip replacement within a year, I realized that TM would have been helpful, but I didn't have time, for during this same period my wife and I decided to sell our Long Island home and relocate closer to our family in Pennsylvania. After physical rehabilitation from the surgeries and our relocation were complete, I was free to return to my meditation routine. Though I needed to de-stress from forty-one years of working and commuting, I was soon comfortable practicing TM again.

Two funny side notes remain from my Transcendental Meditation experience: Big Mike once asked me to reveal my secret mantra. Though this was considered taboo, I revealed my mantra anyway. Surprisingly, our mantras were exactly the same. Was it sheer coincidence? Did Big Mike and I have the same exact personality traits? Or was that the "Mantra of the Day" on Bedford Avenue? Receiving a personalized mantra, especially selected just for you, went up in smoke that day. This coincidence made us laugh whenever the subject of secret mantras was discussed.

One day my daughter and grandkids came by the house to visit us while I, with the door closed to my home office, was deep into my second meditation.

"Grandma, where's Grandpa?"

Tina responded, "He's meditating in his office."

They then asked her, "How high off the ground does he get when he levitates?"

My meditation abruptly ended at that point because I couldn't control my laughter. As radio and TV personality Art Linkletter would always remind us, "Kids say the darndest things."

By the way, I think I have always remained on the ground during my meditation sessions.

CHAPTER THIRTY-SIX

Time to Work

After two challenging years of study, I successfully completed all my classes and exams, earning a Bachelor of Arts degree in economics from Brooklyn College. Several factors contributed to this achievement: the unwavering support of my family, the resourcefulness instilled by my Brooklyn upbringing, guidance from a respected sociology professor, and the assistance and creative writing of my friend Murray. Beyond the degree itself, I also gained a lifelong soulmate during my time at college.

With college now in my rear-view mirror, it was time to go off to work and earn a living. Returning to that same F train that had taken me to high school, Coney Island, NBC Studios at Rockefeller Center, Gimbels, and the Borough of Manhattan Community College, I was now commuting to the 23rd Street Station in Manhattan. Thanks to that sergeant in the National Guard, I was ready to report to duty at First National City Bank, which would later change its name to Citibank. On February 14, 1977, Valentine's Day, my first day of work would be at a branch located on the corner of Avenue of the Americas and 23rd Street, right in the heart of the Toy District now referred to as the Flatiron District. I asked to speak to the manager, Robert Conlin. A veteran banker, Bob had spent his entire career at the bank.

After pleasantries and introductions had been exchanged, I learned about the platform, the area where clerical staff and assistant managers handled customer inquiries and opened accounts. I was hired by a major financial institution with an excellent reputation, although not into their official management-trainee program like some others. This program, designed for graduates of prestigious universities, offered a fast track to management and higher pay. Unlike those candidates, I lacked a formal structure to develop banking skills. Despite this, I was content with the employment opportunity and believed I could perform equally well and eventually attain a management position.

A majority of my coworkers were very kind to me. They did their best to expose me to every phase of branch banking. Unfortunately, there was one assistant manager who was not as considerate. Judging by his attitude and snarky remarks, I sensed he felt threatened by my presence. He had worked for the bank for a number of years and attained the level of assistant manager. He wanted to advance to managerial level but had been bypassed on numerous occasions. Perhaps he had felt his lack of a college degree was holding him back, and people like me were going to jeopardize his future opportunities. However, I think his thought process was totally misguided. Probably the real reason he was being bypassed was because he was a real jerk. One time when it was just the two of us on the platform, I asked him a question while I was dealing with a customer.

His answer was, "You have a college degree, figure it out for yourself." That would be the last time I ever asked him for help. And I eventually did figure it out.

I spent the first six months of my banking career at that location, and for the most part, it was enjoyable. Most of my coworkers were very nice and knowledgeable. They did their best to train me and make me feel welcome. My only complaint was having to eat lunch at 10:30 a.m. every day. Mine was the time slot for rookies, I guess. Who eats lunch at 10:30 a.m.? Well, I did for a very long time.

One day, eating by myself, I noticed no one came down at 11:00 a.m. for their lunch break. By 11:30, I thought the situation was odd with my being the only person in the lunchroom. I walked up the stairs to the main banking floor to find that the entire bank was empty. Standing across the street were all my coworkers with other pedestrians. There also were several police cars and fire trucks parked outside the bank in a scene reminiscent of a *Twilight Zone* episode.

Back in the seventies, New York City experienced many bomb incidents for which the Puerto Rican freedom fighters, or FALN, took responsibility. Apparently, one such threat happened that very day at my work location. I guess my coworkers forgot about the rookie in the lunchroom. They were all frantically yelling and waving to me to leave the bank immediately. I exited stage left (sorry for the *Snagglepuss* cartoon reference) and ran across the street to join them. They were all very apologetic for having left me behind.

The bomb squad entered the bank, and thank goodness, no explosives were found. Days after this incident, some of my coworkers were retelling the story in the lunchroom. I had no clue about bomb threats to financial institutions. One coworker asked whether I had ever heard about what had happened at Fraunces Tavern. I had heard about that bombing from both newspaper accounts and television reports in 1975. That correlation between a historic landmark that once was headquarters for George Washington and my bank branch in the Toy District somehow escaped me. Yet this incident seemed to be one of many in an ongoing situation common among banks in the seventies and early eighties. Probably events like this went right over my head because I was too busy filing down bingo chips into little dimes or trying to win a hand in Spades at school. Experiencing an armed robbery was my main concern working at a retail bank. Thankfully, I never got to experience robbers entering the bank with their weapons drawn as depicted in the movie *Dog Day Afternoon*.

I did get to experience another bomb threat, though, within four months of my first one. Having been sent to our satellite branch on Ninth Avenue and 24th Street, which only had six employees, I was to assist when the staff was shorthanded. On this day I would be assisting two tellers and the bank manager. When the manager had to leave for a meeting, I was left in charge of the bank. With my Brooklyn bravado, I felt confident all would be well.

The bank wasn't busy, and the tellers were managing the customer traffic, while I, a trainee with limited banking experience, remained on the platform alone. Soon an elderly woman who spoke little English approached me and said, "Bag ticky-ticky." She repeated herself as she pointed to a brown paper bag at the check-writing counter on the banking floor.

I moved toward the counter, and I heard something ticking inside the bag. I immediately ran to the tellers, told them to lock their drawers, and escorted everyone out of the bank. Outside, I used a payphone to call the police. The bomb squad, police, and fire engines arrived within minutes, as did the bank manager. He was astonished to see what had transpired during his short absence. The bomb squad entered the bank and found an old alarm clock in that paper bag. Order was restored, and the bank would eventually be reopened. However, my heart was racing, ticky-ticky, until we locked our doors for the final time that day.

After spending the first six months of my banking career in the Toy District, I was transferred Uptown. My new branch location would be on Broadway and 40th Street in the heart of Garment Center. I would spend the next eight years of my career at that location. Once again, I would be traveling on the F train, now two stops further into Manhattan, from 23rd Street to 42nd Street. There are thirty-six different subway lines shuttling passengers across Manhattan, Queens, Brooklyn, and the Bronx.

Somehow, I always found myself traveling for pleasure, school, or work on the F train line.

Not until my promotion to branch manager did my commuting by public transportation on the F train end. My first assignment as branch manager was in Lower Manhattan on William and John Streets. The F train wasn't near that location or any of the subsequent locations where I would later be employed.

The last twenty-three years of my banking career I was commuting by car to Queens. My new train line would be the 7 train to Shea Stadium or Citi Field, to catch a Mets Opening Day game. I had some familiarity with the 7 line as I consistently attended Opening Day for the Mets while in high school, college, and during my working career.

CHAPTER THIRTY-SEVEN

Son of Sam

In April 1977 after a year hiatus, Tina and I started dating again. Our parents were accepting of our rekindled romance and things were going well. During our courtship another phenomenon was taking place in New York City. The Son of Sam, whose real name was David Berkowitz, had been terrorizing New Yorkers since 1976. After using a hunting knife for his first few attacks, he switched to a .44 caliber Bulldog revolver. His victims were mostly young women in the Bronx, Brooklyn, and Queens, though in a few cases he also shot the men they were with. In four cases, the victims were sitting in parked cars. Overall, this serial killer was involved in eight New York City shootings between July 1976 and July 1977. He killed six people and wounded seven others during this period. He was arrested in August 1977 and pleaded guilty to all his crimes.

During the Son of Sam crime wave, Tina's mom didn't want us going out in the evening. Many of our dates were in the neighborhood, during the daytime hours. Our evenings would be spent watching television in Tina's basement. Ordering Chinese takeout, we'd catch an old movie or see a Knicks game, which Tina reluctantly agreed to watch. Though I understood her mom's concern, we disliked losing our freedom at this time in our courtship. We were young and used to going places and doing things. There would be plenty of time for us to sit in front of a TV in the future, when we were older and married.

On July 30, 1977, Tina and I had to go out for the evening.

Our friends Peter and Beth were getting married that night. My future mother-in-law was not thrilled with this inevitable event we had to attend. The affair lasted into the wee hours of the night into the next day. Early that morning, on July 31, the Son of Sam preyed on his last victims—Stacy Moskowitz and Robert Violante in a parked car in Bath Beach, Brooklyn. Firing four rounds into the car, he struck both Stacy and Robert. Robert lost his left eye, and Stacy died from her injuries some eighteen hours later.

As reports aired almost immediately, Tina's mom watched in horror. All she remembered hearing was a blonde Jewish girl and her Italian boyfriend had been shot that night. Thinking we could have been the victims, she was frantic. Totally oblivious to the attack, we arrived at Tina's home. So thankful to see us, her mom showered us in hugs and kisses. This night ended the horrible Son of Sam saga, for he was arrested ten days after that attack. The emotional and physical damage that killer inflicted would be felt in our city and across the country for many years.

Who would have ever thought that such a horrible event could somehow establish a closer bond between my future mother-in-law and me?

CHAPTER THIRTY-EIGHT

𝕮he 𝕭lizzard of 1978

On Sunday, February 5, 1978, and lasting through February 7, the Northeast experienced one of the worst blizzards of the century. The New York City area had a record snowfall of 17.7 inches, the sixth largest snowfall since records had been kept in 1869. The city was in total shutdown mode. Cars on the Brooklyn streets were frozen in blocks of ice within their parking spaces. With very limited bus and train service available, New York City Public Transportation was nearly paralyzed. Mayor Ed Koch closed the New York City school system for three days. Governor Hugh Carey asked President Jimmy Carter to declare "a major disaster" in New York.

Despite the blizzard-like conditions, Tina insisted on keeping our Sunday date. She was in Sheepshead Bay, while my rear-wheel drive Ford Pinto was snowbound in Gravesend, buried further by sanitation efforts. The hours needed to dig it out, coupled with the hazardous drive and likely lack of parking near her place, made me want to cancel. I explained these difficulties to Tina, hoping she would agree, but she remained resolute in her desire to meet.

I recall that Sheepshead Bay was experiencing the same severe weather as Gravesend. Despite our homes being only three miles apart, the conditions were so treacherous that even Seargeant Preston of the mid-fifties Western *Sergeant Preston of the Yukon* would likely have avoided the journey. Unmoved by my logical reasoning, Tina became restless at home and chose to walk to my house in Gravesend. To this day, forty-eight years later, I remain astonished by her choice.

I was shocked to see her arrive at my door, looking like a frozen popsicle, and my immediate question was, "Where did you park your car?"

"I didn't drive here."

"Did you take a cab?"

"No."

I said, "The buses and trains aren't running. How did you get here?"

Despite the cold, windy weather and our prior discussion, she had walked three miles to see me. (In good weather, this would have been at least a forty-minute walk.) This snowy encounter taught me two things: never underestimate a woman's resolve to see her boyfriend, and all women are a bit crazy!

Following a day of playing cards and watching TV, we had a nice dinner prepared by my mother. Later, I dug my car out and drove Tina home through the snow-covered streets. Parking was predictably difficult in Sheepshead Bay, and I had to leave her at her parents' quickly, hoping they didn't think the snowy get-together was my idea.

Returning to Gravesend, my immediate concern was parking. Fortunately, the spot I had vacated was still available since no one had gone out while I was away. Due to the terrible weather conditions, no sane individual was driving or even walking the streets that day, except for one crazy girl from Sheepshead Bay, who decided to walk over three miles in a blizzard to see her boyfriend.

Considering public sentiment and my own reflection, I recommend we proceed with the insanity plea, your Honor.

CHAPTER THIRTY-NINE

Sheepshead Bay

Sheepshead Bay became my new neighborhood since my honey had lived on East 29th Street between Avenues W and X. I was there practically every day (weather permitting) during our renewed courtship. Taking advantage of everything Sheepshead Bay had to offer, we walked along Emmons Avenue checking out the charter fishing boats and beautiful water views. Our favorite places included Roll-N-Roaster, Shatzkin's Famous Knishes, the El Greco and Sheepshead Bay diners, and Pips Comedy Club. You will notice I left out Joe's Clam Bar, Randazzo's Clam Bar, and Lundy's Restaurant. You can ask my father or Uncle Bennie to refresh your memory of my eating preferences in those days.

Roll-N-Roaster was known for its great roast beef sandwiches, cheese fries, and onion rings. Behind the counter were pretty girls wearing tight white T-shirts with their brown uniforms. Okay, so I didn't only go there for their great food! I was so happy when Tina told me she loved roast beef. We both could enjoy the Roll-N-Roaster experience for our own personal reasons.

After seeing a show at Pips Comedy Club, enjoying a long walk, or seeing a movie, we would often have a meal at one of the Sheepshead Bay diners.

In my early college years, I also went to those diners after a night out clubbing with my Battle House brothers. One night my friend Marty and I went to the Sheepshead Bay Diner after returning from the Salty Dog on Long Island. We were sitting in a booth around three in the morning when suddenly we noticed a ruckus in the parking lot. A few individuals were throwing punches at one another. That, in itself, wasn't an unusual occurrence in the wee hours of the morning in Brooklyn. What made this particular incident unique was the two burly gents sitting in the booth in front of us, who also took notice of the parking lot fight.

When the fight moved near their Cadillac, one guy said to the other, "I'm going outside before these two mamalukes hit my car." With that, he reached into his jacket and started to pull out a revolver.

The other guy said, "Hey, put that thing away, you jackass!"

Marty and I exchanged glances, contemplating whether it was the right moment to resurrect our elementary school duck-and-cover drill. Thankfully, the altercation ended without gunfire, and the *mamalukes*—that's Italian-American slang for "fools or buffoons"—eventually stopped fighting. Marty and I decided that, in the future, we would satisfy our early morning hunger pangs within the confines of our own homes.

When Tina and I were together, we enjoyed seeing the up-and-coming comedians at the Pips Comedy Club. With a reasonable admission price, we saw future rising stars including Billy Crystal, Richard Lewis, Larry David, Elaine Boosler, and Andrew Dice Clay. One of our favorites, David Brenner, engaged the audience by asking for a topic and riffing off the cuff with his humorous quick wit. Pips was Brenner's first regular gig, lasting eighteen months before his appearance on *The Tonight Show Starring Johnny Carson*, where he would eventually appear 158 times. We were fortunate to have seen him in his infancy.

Tina and I enrolled in evening adult-education courses at Sheepshead Bay High School after we got engaged. Tina opted for an Italian cooking class, while I chose calligraphy. Despite already learning the art of Sicilian cooking from Mama Grippa every Sunday morning, Tina felt the need for some extra-credit classes. My interest in calligraphy stemmed from my less than stellar penmanship and cursive writing skills. Had I remained in Catholic school, this class might not have been necessary, but we all remember how that experience turned out.

I was hopeful that I could master the art of calligraphy in time for addressing envelopes for our engagement and wedding announcement cards. Once a week Tina and I would grab a bite to eat in her neighborhood and then walk to her alma mater for our night classes. One school night, which happened to be Halloween, I was too ill to attend class. I asked Tina to stay home as I was concerned about her walking alone to class that night. Of course, she decided to go against my wishes.

Unfortunately, she encountered a few young boys who saw her as an easy target for their tomatoes. Despite her having run as fast as she could, one of the tomatoes hit her square in the back. When she arrived at school, she told her teacher she needed to return home to change. Tina then called me to come and get her. Still sick, I got out of bed, picked her up at school, and took her home. I maintained my track record of dating girls who were not as fast as me or Adeline for that matter. The only difference about this Halloween experience was that tomatoes rather than eggs were airborne.

Tina enjoyed her cooking class and was given an Italian cookbook by her instructor as a pre-wedding present, complete with a personal inscription. Despite this comprehensive cookbook, which included various Italian dishes, she primarily cooked Mama Grippa's recipes after we married. It's worth noting that the cooking class focused on general Italian cuisine, not specifically Sicilian dishes.

CHAPTER FORTY
Tying the Knot

Tina and I married in October 1979. Excluding our one-year separation, we had dated nearly three years. With her father already on board, Tina's mom came to terms with our impending marriage. My parents, too, also became comfortable with our decision as they got to know and like Tina. Their relationship strengthened when Tina started spending Sunday mornings in my mother's kitchen learning how to cook my favorite meals and the "Sauce" of course. Yes, it's *sauce*, not *gravy*!

Before Tina attended our first Sunday dinner, I offered tips on the proper etiquette at Mama Grippa's dining room table. Tina would have to help set the table, clean up after our meal, and offer to help in the kitchen. Knowing full well my mother wouldn't have trusted anyone with her pots and pans, Tina could pass on that chore. I had to make it perfectly clear to her that my Sicilian mother would be watching her every move. I had learned this from prior experience, when another girl I dated didn't lift a finger to help. My mother went on and on about that episode for quite some time. I wasn't stupid. I wanted this relationship to flourish, and so did Tina. Did all these pre-dinner instructions intimidate my future wife? Maybe a little. She was, however, determined to make a good first impression with my family and, more importantly, my mother.

Most twenty-two-year-old girls would have probably told me to take a hike after all of these instructions, but she didn't. Tina embraced them. I guess that's what love is all about.

Tina proved to be both a capable student and an excellent cook, mastering all my mother's recipes and perfecting her sauce. Given her academic success, her aptitude in the kitchen shouldn't have been unexpected. However, her ability to interpret my mother's verbal recipes, which were characterized by vague measurements like "a pinch of this" or "a handful of that" depending on the portion, was truly remarkable. It's hard to imagine learning from an instructor who gave instructions in such an imprecise way. Additionally, my mother was a whirlwind in the kitchen. As Tina would jot down her notes, my mother, tossing ingredients into a pot at a record pace, was usually three ingredients ahead of her.

Looking over Tina's notations after one of her culinary sessions, I noticed a tablespoon and a half of "white stuff" listed as an ingredient. I asked her, "What the heck is "white stuff?" She pointed to the Crisco All Vegetable Shortening on the kitchen counter. After that revelation, I was amazed that she had been able to replicate any of my mother's dishes, but Tina did and still does to this day.

Despite their different ethnic backgrounds, our parents shared surprising common ground, likely stemming from shared moral principles, family values, and histories of hardship and prejudice.

Growing up in Brooklyn with many Jewish friends, I observed firsthand the cultural similarities, particularly the emphasis on strong family structures and shared beliefs. Both our families were hardworking, middle class, and deeply committed to their children's well-being. Perhaps unsurprisingly, they also both appreciated good Italian food. The only difference was my family's preference for making our Italian meals instead of eating them in a restaurant. The final common denominator we all shared was growing up and living in Brooklyn.

As our families started spending more time together, we

realized that we shared some mutual acquaintances. Uncle Bennie from Long Island and my father-in-law, Bert, had mutual friends who worked at JFK International Airport. My uncle was a Port Authority Police Officer who had spent a number of years at the airport. My father-in-law owned a gas station on Flushing and Knickerbocker Avenues in Brooklyn. He serviced many vehicles that came from that airport. They discovered at one of our get-togethers that they had several mutual close friends. When I was working in Queens, I brought my car in for servicing at a local gas station near my job. The two owners of the service station came highly recommended by my coworkers. One owner was Jewish, the other Puerto Rican. I mentioned to them that my Jewish father-in-law also had a Puerto Rican partner at his service station in Brooklyn. Almost instantly one partner said, "Is your father-in-law's name Bert?"

After responding, the man revealed to me that Bert had given him his first opportunity at his gas station in Brooklyn. What a small world.

Now that our families had become acquainted, our next challenge would be preparing for our upcoming wedding. Tina and I went to great lengths to consider our parents' feelings with our wedding plans. Rather than marry in a church or in a synagogue, we chose to say our "I do's" at the reception venue. A reformed rabbi would perform the ceremony, with a Catholic priest present for the blessing. Tina and I felt this unifying approach would be accepted by both families.

Before our engagement, Tina and I had decided that our children would be raised Catholic, while exposing them to the Jewish faith and customs. One of the prerequisites of marrying with the church's blessing was our having to attend a Pre-Cana marriage preparation course at St. Simon and Jude Church. Surprisingly, my in-laws had to become involved in the process. As adults, Tina and I were puzzled by this requirement. My in-laws graciously complied with the pastor's request, a gesture that I would always appreciate and never forget.

Through both our completion of the Pre-Cana course and commitment to rear our children in the Catholic faith, our wedding, a convalidation ceremony, though performed by a rabbi, was recognized and blessed by the Church as a valid sacramental marriage.

Because the rabbi had once been affiliated with a synagogue in Rome, Italy, he was fluent in Italian. After the ceremony and traditional glass breaking, the rabbi said a few words in Italian. That was a pleasant surprise to all in attendance.

The reception took place at Terrace on the Park on the old 1964 World's Fair site at Flushing Meadows Corona Park, in Queens, New York. Though the food was good, the music from our live band was even better. My sister-in-law, Sue, performed with the band to sing our wedding song "For All We Know" by the Carpenters. Unlike the Revel Tones from earlier days, this group was also well versed in performing "Hava Nagila" and the "Tarantella." Though ours turned out to be a perfect evening, the same couldn't be said for Cousin Vinny, who's car had been stolen in the parking lot.

Flying to Aruba the next morning for our honeymoon, we spent one week at the beautiful Americana Hotel. During the day, we enjoyed the pristine, white sandy beaches and turquoise waters. We toured the island by moped and watched the Divi-Divi trees blowing in the wind. After dinner, we visited the casino on the premises.

Tina wasn't eager to gamble, but I enjoyed every table and slot machine available. My newlywed wife became a little concerned with my new appreciation for gambling. By the last day of our stay, I had just enough money for cab fare to the airport.

To our surprise on our last night in Aruba, we ran into friends from Brooklyn College, who were also heading home the next day. Agreeing to split cab fare, I now had an opportunity to return to the casino to make my final deposit. Arriving at JFK airport with empty pockets, I called my brother, Vinny, to rescue us at the parking lot. Tina's look that day was enough to reform this one-time degenerate gambler into never spending beyond his means again. In time she realized I could be a responsible gambler, and there would be no need for a second mortgage. I learned some valuable lessons on my honeymoon: Do everything in moderation, and it's okay to have some fun gambling. Just make sure to have enough money for cab fare and the parking lot.

Prior to our marriage Tina and I planned to save for a down payment on a house. Since teaching jobs in 1978 were scarce, Tina secured a full-time clerical position at Lafayette Electronics in Syosset, New York. To avoid a long commute, she stayed at my aunt and uncle's house in Lindenhurst. Imagine Tina making this commitment before we were married. My girl had chutzpah! Boro Park strikes again. I worked two full-time jobs for a year to add to our down payment goal. Soon after I graduated college, another national guardsman referred me to Standard & Poor's for a nighttime clerical position. Not too long after that, I secured my daytime position at First National City Bank. Chasing our American Dream, both Tina and I endured long days and nights.

After our honeymoon, we settled into our new life on Long Island because we couldn't afford a house in Brooklyn, and I didn't want to live in an apartment. We purchased a starter home in Dix Hills, New York, before our marriage. We spent every day off and weekend painting and cleaning that house for our eventual occupancy.

Now considered Long Islanders, we felt a drastic change in our lives. No longer traveling a short ride on the F train from Kings Highway to Midtown anymore, I would be commuting to the city via the Long Island Railroad. I had to factor in time to drive to the station and the extra time for my longer walk from Penn Station to the Garment Center.

Working for United Cerebral Palsy, Tina secured a special education teaching position on the East End of Long Island. Heading east not west, as I and millions of other commuters did, she traveled a reverse Long Island commute. We both would experience much longer workdays and weekends than we anticipated. I'm not complaining; home ownership would prove to be one of the best decisions we had ever made. We just never considered the extraordinary toll and impact it would have on us.

We would always remind one another of that famous quote from Hyman Roth in *The Godfather Part II* when he said, "This is the business we've chosen." Well, this was the life we had chosen.

Even though we had relocated to Long Island as first time homeowners, we never officially left Brooklyn, for we both had our parents, other family members, and friends still there as well as our commitment to share traditional Sunday afternoon meals with my family.

CHAPTER FORTY-ONE

RETURNING TO OUR BROOKLYN ROOTS

As newlyweds, we found little time for social activities on Long Island. Saturdays were devoted to cleaning, laundry, grocery shopping, lawn care, and other home projects needing attention. On Sundays, we made our weekly pilgrimage to Brooklyn via the Southern State and Belt Parkways. We stopped first in Sheepshead Bay to visit with Tina's parents and then headed over to Gravesend for that afternoon meal with my parents, Sue, Vinny, and nephew Michael. We also tried to occasionally squeeze in visits with friends who were still living in Brooklyn.

One late Sunday afternoon while visiting my parents, Tina and I walked along Ocean Parkway, a boulevard running north to south from Prospect Park Circle to Brighton Beach, about five and a half miles in length. The width of Ocean Parkway includes six lanes of automobile traffic, with walking and bicycling paths on both sides of the street. These beautiful tree-lined paths, which we often enjoyed, also had park benches situated from one end to the other. Completed in 1876, this boulevard is lined with single-family homes, mansions, and apartment buildings.

While walking that day, we were heading in the direction of Brighton Beach when an older man was coming toward us on his bicycle. Immediately I recognized him to be Mr. Schepps, my old economics teacher from Lincoln High School. I spoke to him without getting much of a reaction and filled him in on my life after high school. Perhaps because I had cut so many of his classes, he simply didn't remember me. Nevertheless, I was grateful for the opportunity to thank him again for giving me a passing grade in his class. I wanted him to know that his decision had been sound. In our once-in-a-lifetime chance meeting, I enjoyed seeing him riding his same bicycle twelve years later. He was a man living by his principles.

Seeing our family and friends was always our top priority when visiting Brooklyn. On many of those return trips, we made sure to visit places that had a special meaning to us. We would drive to Boro Park so Tina could see where I grew up. Then we would drive to Bensonhurst where Tina's childhood began. After seeing our old apartment buildings and the surrounding areas, we would head to our favorite hangouts in Brooklyn. L&B Spumoni Gardens was always first on our list of places to go. When we lived in Brooklyn, that was a favorite place to enjoy a pizza and their homemade spumoni and Italian ices. We also enjoyed visiting Cuccio's Bakery, the Foursome, El Greco and Sheepshead Bay Diners, Roll-N-Roaster, Butter Bun Bake Shop, Shatkins Knishes, Seniors, Silver Star Restaurant, Smolinski's Delicatessen (owned by Tina's great uncle), and Nathan's Famous, to name just a few.

We loved going back in time, seeing our old neighborhoods, and sampling our favorite Brooklyn cuisines.

CHAPTER FORTY-TWO

My in-Laws Leave Brooklyn for Arizona

My in-laws left Brooklyn for the warmer climate of Phoenix, Arizona, after my father-in-law Bert retired in 1981. They wanted to be near their oldest daughter, Nadine; her husband, Marty; and their two young children, Sean and Fara. Additionally, their son, Alan; daughter-in-law, Janet; and their son, Heith, were currently residing in California, which was a short plane ride away. They knew that Tina was in good and capable hands with my family. She would receive all the love and support needed in helping us raise our family.

Now instead of us seeing my in-laws in Sheepshead Bay on our Sunday trips, they would be visiting us on Long Island during their semiannual cross-country trips. Since they still had friends and family living there, returning to Brooklyn was always part of their itinerary.

I soon learned that my mother-in-law was a sweet, caring person. Her migraines suddenly dissipated after she realized her daughter wasn't marrying a mafia don. My father-in-law had always treated me well since our initial meeting in his home. Their tolerance and acceptance of our premarital church obligations was an indication of their great moral fiber.

My father-in-law, who had a quirky personality, was a generous person who always liked treating us to dinner. He was unfamiliar with Long Island and would have to rely on us for restaurant suggestions. When he lived in Brooklyn, we always ate at Seniors Restaurant on Nostrand Avenue. There, he was treated like one of the characters on *Cheers* where everyone knew his name.

His quirky personality was evident one evening when Tina and I invited him to one of our favorite Long Island restaurants. As soon as he sat down at the table, he asked the waitress, "May I have a glass of water?"

The waitress brought it.

"Can I get a slice of lemon with that?"

After she brought the lemon, he asked, "Do you have any Sweet'N Low?"

She returned with the sweetener.

"Can I get a glass of ice on the side?" Then, after taking a few sips of water, he asked for a refill.

The poor waitress needed roller skates to handle all his beverage and food requests. Just watching their interaction, I became exhausted. Embarrassed, Tina and I decided to invite him to restaurants where the staff was unfamiliar with us. Though Dad was curious about our long drives to restaurants outside of our zip code, he accepted our explanation of wanting to experience new places. I'm sure there were waitresses in Montauk and the North Fork who probably dreaded seeing us walk through the door.

Another quirk was Dad's love for early morning baths just when I needed to use the bathroom and leave for work. Every morning during his entire stay, my home's only bathroom with a shower was off limits to me; I missed my commuter train every morning thanks to his newfound bathing habits. Wanting to avoid a confrontation, I asked, to no avail, both Tina and her mother for help. One good result, however, did occur. I became motivated to buy a home with multiple bathrooms. Not surprisingly, after we had moved, he never took another long morning bath in any one of those bathrooms when I was rushing off to work.

This next story about dear old Dad is the epitome of his quirky personality. On one visit to Long Island, he arrived at our home with an old, heavy nineteen-inch television set. Of course, I thought he was gifting the television to us for our spare bedroom. A logical thought since we had no television in the room where my in-laws slept. I soon learned that the television was broken, and he wanted me to return it to a store in Manhattan where he had purchased it.

I said, "Dad, how am I going to carry it on the railroad and then the subway?"

"I was able to get it here from Arizona; I'm sure you can manage to take it with you to the city," he responded.

"Do you have a sales receipt for this TV?" I asked.

"No, son, but when you get there, just mention my name, the owner knows me, and he will replace it."

This television, at least five years old and without a receipt, was not, in my estimation, going to be repaired or replaced. I asked Tina and her mother to intervene again on my behalf and work on making the return themselves.

The next morning the television was on my kitchen table, with a note attached that read, "Thanks, Son." It remained there for a few days until Dad finally got the message. He took the television back to the city, and I never saw it again. Since we didn't discuss it when he returned, I suspect he didn't get a refund for that old TV.

Dad had another rather eccentric request. Whenever he visited, he wanted me to take him to the Beth Moses Cemetery in West Babylon, New York. Since he had a pre-paid cemetery plot provided by the Arista Lodge in Brooklyn for both his wife and himself, he reminded me where the two would rest eternally. Though his desire to reinforce my knowledge of his plans during every visit seemed unnecessary to me, Tina and I certainly honored those wishes years later. Whenever we return to Long Island to pay our respects, I am always reminded of my father-in-law's final wishes. In fact, because of all the trips we made together, I think I can find that gravesite with my eyes closed.

CHAPTER FORTY-THREE

The Brooklyn Honeymoon Was Over

As much as Tina and I enjoyed going back to Brooklyn every Sunday to see our family and friends, it became more challenging with the arrival of our daughter, Elizabeth, and Tina carrying our second child. Sitting idly on Sunday evenings on the Belt Parkway in a compact car filled with baby paraphernalia, a baby girl and her expectant Mommy past their naptimes, the drive was beginning to take its toll on all of us.

Since Tina's parents had moved to Arizona and with many of our relatives now living on Long Island, I asked my parents to consider a relocation. There were only a few relatives and paisanos from Sicily still living in Brooklyn at that time. My father seemed open to the suggestion, but my mother was adamant about not leaving "Brook a lean." She would argue that if she moved to Long Island, her whole life would be turned upside down. Besides dealing with all that comes with a house sale and purchase, she would have to change doctors, lose the ability to walk to stores, and miss seeing her childhood friends from Francavilla. I tried to reassure her that my brother and I would assist with the move, find her a home near us, and help her acclimate to her new surroundings; however, she wouldn't budge.

I then suggested that she could visit us every weekend or come during the week since both of my parents were retired. They also had the option of spending time with my brother or with us because we both had ample accommodations. My mother's response to that was, "Your father likes to sleep in his own bed."

At a stalemate with her, I reached the point of no return. If she wanted to see her grandchildren, Mom would have to come to Long Island. Until my children were older, my long Sunday drives on the Belt Parkway were over. My mother didn't speak to me for several weeks after missing our first Sunday gathering. Her obstinance, however, was defeated by her desire to be with her grandchildren. She decided to put her home on the market, which sold fairly quickly. My brother and I located a modest three-bedroom ranch, which was in walking distance between our homes. With help from us, the transition from one home to another went smoothly. We would now experience a lifestyle similar to the one my family enjoyed in Brooklyn. We could now see each other during the week and enjoy our Sunday meals together.

One evening after visiting my parents, we noticed a "For Sale" sign on a home near their residence. The owners were outside, and I asked if we could possibly tour their home. They let us in, and Tina and I fell in love with it. We already had a familiarity with the layout since my brother had an identical home around the corner.

It was a four-bedroom colonial with two and a half baths, a basement, fireplace, and, in the backyard, an inground swimming pool. With a second child on the way and my in-laws' visiting us more frequently, we needed a larger home—especially one with multiple baths to accommodate my father-in-law. After talking it over with my wife, we made the owners an offer they couldn't refuse. I always wanted to say that line. This is what happens when you've seen *The Godfather* a thousand times.

Having negotiated on a price throughout the evening, after midnight I returned to the owners' home with a good faith check.

Our attorneys prepared contracts early the next day. Our next hurdle now was to immediately sell our house. Since paying for an agent was cost prohibitive, I placed an advertisement in *Newsday's* real estate section. Unfortunately, though bombarded with calls (mostly from real estate agents) nothing materialized. With less than a month before our closing date, Tina and I found ourselves wondering, "What did we get ourselves into?" We said this to each other almost every night in bed. Tina could have easily said the old Laurel and Hardy line, "Here's another fine mess you've gotten me into." Thankfully, she had never watched any of their movies.

To our great relief, once again, a Brooklyn connection came through for us with our *Newsday* ad placement. A Bensonhurst couple had saved our two-month-old advertisement and decided to call. After they saw our home, they made us an offer we couldn't refuse.

Once the purchase was completed, we would go on to become good friends with Danny and Karen. In time, the Brooklyn connection with our new friends became even stronger. Paralleling each other's lives, Danny and I, both Italian, were from Brooklyn. Our banking careers began in Manhattan with a large commercial bank. We lived in our Long Island homes for thirty-four years, both with two children who attended the same schools. We also made home alterations to accommodate aging parents. Later in our lives, we sold our homes within weeks of each other to be near a daughter and her family. It was striking to have all these similarities. Danny loved *The Godfather* movies, too.

With plenty of space for our growing family and guests, we were fortunate to have my parents nearby. They would assist us with getting the kids on and off the school bus and stay with them when they were ill or had an abbreviated school schedule. My parents' help allowed Tina to return to work as a full-time teacher. No longer homesick for Brooklyn, my parents, who adored their grandchildren, now filled their days with purpose.

Our new home, the center of our universe, served as a family gathering place and our children's meeting place for playdates. Both the basketball hoop on the side of the house and an inground swimming pool in the backyard saw plenty of activity. In addition, our finished basement became the hub for indoor recreational games with friends and family.

While the boys were occupied with their soldiers, dinosaurs, and video games, the girls played with their dolls and dollhouses and toy kitchen appliances. When everyone played together, I recalled my experiences at Tommy's house in Boro Park when I was a child. My kids just needed a stickball bat and *Spaldeen* for it to be a true Brooklyn experience.

CHAPTER FORTY-FOUR

Finding My Faith Again

Following my sixth-grade experiences at St. Frances de Chantal, I grew disillusioned with the Catholic Church. This led me to refuse to attend Sunday services with my parents at our new parish, Sts. Simon and Jude, after we moved to Gravesend. Given my background in parochial school, I suspect my parents anticipated my eventual return to church attendance. Though I had always believed in God and prayed daily, I attended mass only on Easter and Christmas. I couldn't bring myself to attend mass on a regular basis since it always brought back bad memories.

Of course, when Tina and I had started planning a future together, I had to reconsider my connection to my faith. She wanted our children exposed to both religions. She also hoped we would celebrate all our religious holidays. Not as well versed in her Jewish faith as I was in Catholicism, she agreed that our children should observe the Catholic faith. We both knew that her parents would be more accepting of our religious choices than my family. Our serious discussions certainly had made our engagement, wedding, and family plans much easier than they would have been otherwise.

Rather than bring me closer to the church, having my future in-laws involved in the Pre-Cana process before the course began infuriated me. The pastor would not allow us to attend the class until my in-laws met with him and acknowledged our decision of raising our children in the Catholic faith. It almost seemed like he was asking them to intervene with our marriage plans if they weren't onboard with our decision. This interrogation further increased my bitterness toward the church.

This religious bias wasn't only one sided. Weeks before our wedding, Tina reached out to the rabbi with some last-minute questions and concerns about our upcoming ceremony. Since the rabbi wasn't available, an alternate responded with, "Well you made your bed, now you'll have to lie in it!" Imagine a spiritual leader saying something like this to a future young bride.

When Tina informed me about her discussion with the rabbi's associate, I called to express my feelings about how he had handled the situation. Soon after that, our rabbi called Tina to apologize. He said, "Not everyone is onboard with interfaith marriages, but he should have never made that comment to you." Tina accepted his apology, but this episode just added to my bad feelings about both religions.

In the end, we overcame all of the religious obstacles we faced early in our marriage. Our children grew up with a good understanding of both faiths even though they had a formal education in one. When they both married, they had to make religious choices of their own. I'd like to think their upbringing better prepared them for those decisions.

Because of my past experiences with members of the clergy, I still was having a tough time with my feelings toward religion. When my daughter, Elizabeth, was preparing for her first Holy Communion, she asked if I would be receiving Communion with her. Elizabeth's request brought back memories of Uncle Ben's participation in my confirmation. He was honored to be my sponsor and play such an important role in my life that day. Through my young daughter, I decided to return to the church as an active participant. After going to confession, I participated in Elizabeth's ceremony and received Holy Communion on her special day. I knew then that I may have blamed the church for the behaviors of a few bad actors.

For thirty-five years, my renewed faith has helped me to cope with life's challenges. It has brought me peace, comfort, and the hope of better things to come. Having my grandchildren beside me in church fills me with great joy and a sense of accomplishment.

Having rediscovered my faith, perhaps Sister X and I won't be in the same fiery place after all. It's even possible we might meet in heaven; if God can forgive me, surely, He has forgiven her by now. In any case, our next encounter should be in a much cooler location—assuming St. Peter meets her at the Pearly Gates and takes away her collection of metal rulers, pointers, erasers, and cat o' nine tails.

CHAPTER FORTY-FIVE

Maintaining Brooklyn Friendships

I'm pretty sure there are a lot of people my age who still have some childhood friends they see or communicate with on a fairly regular basis. Maintaining long-term relationships is not unique to growing up in Brooklyn. For some unexplained reason, it seems to me that people who grew up in Brooklyn remain in contact with many more of their childhood friends than people from other areas. I don't have any scientific data to support this theory, only some thoughts to offer.

Maybe it was the sheer number of people we encountered during our early years growing up in a very large city that created a unique scenario for relationships to develop and be maintained. Perhaps it was the social and communication skills we learned early on that helped us maintain our friendships. Or maybe it was our shared Brooklyn experiences that helped develop our common bond. I believe it's a combination of all these things as to why I feel Brooklyn friendships are lasting friendships. Through my having both served in the military and traveled the country for business and pleasure, I have met many people who are often surprised by my numerous Brooklyn friendships that have endured through sixty years.

Even my own children, who grew up on Long Island and have many childhood friends, are mystified by the sheer number of Brooklyn friends I still remain in contact with.

MAINTAINING BROOKLYN FRIENDSHIPS

Few of my Brooklyn childhood friends still live there, with most having moved away after marriage due to housing costs, family, or job prospects. While most stayed within the Tri-State area, some pursued opportunities in the South and West Coast. Despite the distances, many of us have returned to Brooklyn for holidays to visit family and friends. Although getting together became harder over time, we maintained contact through calls, emails, and texts.

I can't explain why most of us all feel compelled to keep this friendship phenomenon going. Is it a fluke or is it a Brooklyn thing? Whatever the reason, I am so grateful for these incredible friendships that I have been lucky to maintain over my lifetime. Every time we get together, be it at reunions in Las Vegas or Florida, or local events with our spouses, we are instantly transformed into the youngsters we once were. Oh, to be eighteen again!

Nothing is better than enjoying each other's company and reliving events we participated in on our city streets, in our schoolyards, in our public schools, or on the campus of Brooklyn College. What a wonderful feeling it is getting into that Time Machine, which transports us all back to the good old days of growing up in Brooklyn.

CHAPTER FORTY-SIX

Brooklyn's Untold Benefits

Growing up in Brooklyn, I often ponder how my life might have unfolded differently elsewhere. W. Clement Stone's assertion that "You are a product of your environment" resonates with me. I consider whether my Brooklyn upbringing facilitated my achievements, shaped my character, and contributed to my social ease. Traveling between boroughs by train at age thirteen, for instance, might have accelerated my maturity. Aligning with Stone's viewpoint, I believe my environment significantly influenced me. Furthermore, I contemplate the extent to which my parents' lives in Brooklyn have shaped who I am.

Growing up in a nurturing family and environment, I recognize my good fortune. Brooklyn, my first home, shaped my values, beliefs, and ambitions. I am certain that Brooklyn has been instrumental in making me the man I am today.

Sigmund Freud's theory of personality, his psychodynamic theory, suggests we are influenced by childhood experiences and social factors. Freud's idea is that what happens to us as kids and the culture we are raised in really shapes who we become. I think it's pretty clear that the people we meet and the situations we go through in life have a huge impact on how we act and feel.

Basically, I'm saying that where we grow up and what happens to us as kids really make us who we are. Brooklyn definitely did that for me. I'm a total product of Brooklyn, and I consider it a huge part of my identity. This hypothesis about Brooklyn might not perfectly align with Sigmund Freud's theories, but what would he know about Brooklyn anyway? He grew up in Austria.

CHAPTER FORTY-SEVEN

Brooklyn's Famous

As promised in the introduction to this book, here are my list and comments, in no particular order, of the people, locations, landmarks, food, beverages, inventions, companies, our Brooklyn accent and weather, that I think contributed to making Brooklyn famous. Forgive me for any oversights. If you want a further glimpse into the glory of Brooklyn, you can research any one of these people, places, and things.

Brooklyn's Famous Comedians

Mel Brooks
Jerry Seinfeld
Richard Lewis
Joan Rivers
Larry David
Henny Youngman
Jerry Stiller
Andrew Dice Clay
Anne Meara
Jimmy Kimmel
Chris Rock
Jackie Gleason
Buddy Hackett
Eddie Murphy
Woody Allen
Pat Cooper
Jimmy Fallon
Adam Sandler
Tracy Morgan
The Three Stooges, Moe, Curly, and Shemp Howard*

*Sorry, Larry and the "Joe's" (Besser and DeRita) were not born or raised in Brooklyn. Couldn't you tell? Although Larry could have easily been mistaken for a Brooklynite.

Brooklyn's Famous Actors and Performers

Barbra Streisand
Anne Hathaway
Lena Horne
Zero Mostel
Marisa Tomei
Mickey Rooney
Barry Manilow
Neil Sedaka (Lincoln HS graduate)
John Forsythe (Lincoln HS graduate)
Rita Hayworth
Jay-Z
Neil Diamond (Lincoln HS graduate)
Debbie Gibson
Alyssa Milano
Rosie Perez
Tony Danza
Harvey Fierstein
Lou Ferrigno
Scott Baio
Barbra Stanwyck
Wolfman Jack
Richie Havens
Edie Falco
Steve Buscemi
Lil' Kim
Veronica Lake
Harvey Keitel
Leah Remini
Jimmy Smits
Larry King
Abe Vigoda
Paul Sorvino
Vic Damone
Rhea Perlman
Louis Gossett, Jr. (Lincoln HS graduate)
Priscilla Presley
Chuck Connors (The Rifleman & Brooklyn Dodger)
Steve Schirripa

Brooklyn's Famous Athletes and Sports Figures

Michael Jordan
Sandy Koufax (from Boro Park)
Mike Tyson
Joe Torre
Frank Torre
Chris Mullin
Rudy LaRusso
Red Auerbach
Vinny Testaverde
Floyd Patterson
Bernard King

Stephon Marbury (Lincoln HS graduate)
Lee Mazzilli (Lincoln HS graduate)
Billy Cuningham
Carmelo Anthony
Connie Hawkins
Paul Lo Duca
Sid Luckman
Waite Hoyt
Al Davis
Lyle Alzado
Dick Bavetta
Larry Brown
Frank Layden
Vince Lombardi
Johnny Petraglia
Sam Rosen (Rangers broadcaster)
Mark Roth
Nelson Figueroa (Lincoln HS graduate)
Sebastian Telfair (Lincoln HS graduate)
Rico Petrocelli
John Franco
Jim Gordon (Rangers broadcaster)
The Albert Brothers, Al, Marv (Lincoln HS graduate), and Steve

Brooklyn's Famous Locations & Landmarks

The Brooklyn Bridge
Coney Island
Prospect Park
Brooklyn Museum
Fort Greene
Dumbo
Brooklyn Heights Promenade
Dyker Heights
Brooklyn Tabernacle Church
Williamsburg
Green-Wood Cemetery
Park Slope
Verrazano Narrows Bridge
Carroll Gardens
Sheepshead Bay
Grand Army Plaza
Brooklyn Cyclones Baseball MCU Park
Barclays Center (where the new Ebbets Field could have been built)

Brooklyn's Famous Foods, Desserts & Beverages

Bagels
Shatzkin's Knishes
Junior's Cheesecake
Nathan's Famous Hot Dogs
Gino's Italian Ices
Manhattan Special Soda
Polly-O Cheese
Tootsie Rolls
Joyva Candy
Peter Luger's Steaks
Mrs. Stahl's Potato Knishes
Ebinger's Blackout Cake
Pastrami Sandwiches
Brooklyn Egg Creams (said to have been introduced by Jewish immigrant Louis Auster in his Brooklyn candy shop)
Pizza (including my personal favorite, L&B Spumoni Gardens)

Brooklyn's Famous Inventions

Air-Conditioning
Credit Cards
Egg Creams
Teddy Bears
Sweet'N Low
Brillo Pads
Roller Coasters
Tootsie Rolls
Bazooka Bubble Gum
Gretsch Guitars
Benjamin Moore Paints
Twizzlers Licorice
Mr. Potato Head
World's First Children's Museum
Esquire Shoe Polish

Brooklyn's Famous Companies

Pfizer
The Squibb Corp.
Gretsch Guitars
Entenmann's Bakery
Mack Trucks
Minwax
Etsy
Vice Media
Kickstarter
Schaefer Brewery
Leviton Electronics
Benjamin Moore Paints

Polly-O Cheese Company   Domino Sugar
Joyva

Brooklyn's Famous Accent

It is argued by certain experts that the Brooklyn accent lacks uniqueness and is merely a product of the diverse ethnicities and socioeconomic backgrounds that have shaped the New York accent. However, this perspective is vehemently contested. Brooklyn residents possess a discernible mode of speech, which is an indisputable fact.

Brooklyn's Famous Weather

There is nothing famous about Brooklyn's weather. You weren't expecting a real answer here, were you?

* * *

I apologize for any omissions in my Brooklyn's Famous Lists; this is not intended to be a definitive authority on the topic. The names and places I've included hold personal significance, and researching famous alumni from Lincoln High School was fascinating. Sandy Koufax being a fellow Boro Park resident was also interesting to learn.

It's always great returning to Brooklyn enjoying the historic scenery, sampling its famous foods, and seeing old friends.

Epilogue

My dad would always share his memories of growing up on the Lower East Side of New York. He told us stories about playing in the Henry Street Settlement, running track at DeWitt Clinton High School, and swimming in the East River. Local authorities would rope off a section where the children could jump from the rocks along the perimeter right into the river. These are just some of the many stories he told me and my brother over the years. I wish I could go back in time and record or video our discussions about his childhood and adolescent years. Many of his shared memories, never to be revisited, have faded over time. Because of such a loss, I wanted to record my experiences and memories of Brooklyn for my children and grandchildren. Documenting and sharing our early years with our family is important to me. Besides, I wanted to transport my family and others to a simpler lifetime in Brooklyn, a place like no other.

I hope these stories bring back good memories of your younger days. Maybe you'll think about playing street games, going on road trips, hanging out with friends, or attending big family gatherings. If this book helps you remember times like that, I truly hope they're happy memories. I vividly recall many of the memories I wrote down, some with more clarity than others.

While writing, I consciously omitted certain adolescent experiences. These weren't due to any criminal or deliberately careless actions, but rather some foolish mistakes I'd prefer not to share with my children and grandchildren. Let them go through life, experiencing their own dopey and silly things. They don't need Grandpa giving them a head start on stupidity. Life experiences are learning experiences.

I am hopeful my grandkids will be good students and not cut classes like Grandpa did. Let Grandma be their role model for their education. She never missed a class and was an excellent student.

This grandpa has portrayed himself as a juvenile delinquent, unable to sit still in a classroom, and proved to be a challenge for his teachers. I had difficulty dealing with authority figures in school, in the Armed Services, and in the business world. For the record, however, I did eventually graduate college with a Bachelor of Arts degree, I served honorably in the military, and I had a successful banking and financial services career that lasted forty-one years.

My greatest accomplishment is my marriage of over forty-five years to Tina, the love of my life. We are blessed with two caring, and responsible adult children, who in turn have given us three loving and affectionate grandchildren.

My nurturing parents, an older brother who always offered sound advice and guidance, and the street smarts I gained in Brooklyn all contributed to developing my character, work ethic, and ultimately, my success and good fortune.

I am hopeful that you enjoyed reading about my memories and experiences of growing up in Brooklyn. I truly enjoyed writing about them for you and my family.

Thank you for coming along on my journey back in time. Remember, *it all started in Brooklyn!*

Acknowledgments

In writing this memoir, I relied on the recollections of my brother, Vinny, and friends Joe, Marty, Richie, Glenn, and Carlos who helped fill gaps in my memory and confirm my own experiences. While I strived for accuracy in depicting the people and places of my Brooklyn childhood, there may be unintentional errors resulting from the occasional memory lapses common at my age of seventy-two. When direct confirmation wasn't available, I trusted my instincts. I believe this account to be a largely truthful representation of my past.

Throughout the writing process of this book, my wife, Tina, served as my invaluable on-site personal editor, and her teaching expertise proved particularly helpful for a new writer. My son, Rob, and my grandchildren, Lila and James, offered immense encouragement for this project. Rob, with his background in English education, diligently proofread the manuscript and contributed valuable edits and suggestions. Numerous individuals, notably Vinny and my sister-in-law Sue, provided insightful feedback and clarifications. Early drafts of the book were shared with family and friends for proofreading and suggestions. My Battle House brothers were instrumental in helping me remember our Brooklyn College days together.

Special thanks are offered to Joe and Lorene Gagliano, Marty Safdia, Glenn Brown, Richie Adler, Carlos Lamour, Bill Kaplan, Stu Stoller, Brad Balmuth, Barry Ahron, Harvey Stein, Mark

Anesh, Richie (The Rube) Rubin, Bernie Dolington, James Raggi, and Ron Rice for their thoughts and contributions.

My heartfelt appreciation goes to Alice Clabaugh, a retired high school English teacher, for her meticulous reading and insightful editorial contributions that were vital in finalizing this book. Alice, our daughter and son-in-law's neighbor, who, along with her husband, Chuck, have become cherished members of our *famiglia*.

I extend my sincere gratitude to my friend, Brandon Steiner, a true visionary in the sports marketing industry, for dedicating his valuable time to thoroughly read my manuscript and for lending his insightful perspective and eloquent voice to craft the Foreword.

With special acknowledgment to Carol and Gary Rosenberg of The Book Couple for their significant support. Their review of my manuscript and guidance through the publishing process were truly invaluable.

My Photos

My beautiful parents, Maria and Biagio

My handsome dad, who was better looking than George Raft

Nonna and Grandpa on one of their many trips to Sicily

Dad, Mom, Zia Alfia, Grandpa Giuseppe (front row), Grandpa Gaetano (back row), Uncle Benny and Aunt Dolly

Goldie's aquarium

A tree falls on a Pontiac in Brooklyn. My favorite Fire Alarm Pull Box is on the corner in Boro Park.

A family vacation at Peggy Runway Lodge

That's me and Daisy on our roof in Boro Park.

Frank Thomas and Al Jackson on Camera Day
in the old Polo Grounds in 1963

My favorite Mets memorabilia purchase ever!

Sue and Vinny's band. Vinny is the guitarist in the middle.

Aunt Millie and Mom, always in the kitchen

Mom, Nonna, Aunt Lucy, and Aunt Millie

Dad, Nonna, Mom, Aunt Millie, and Uncle Bennie

Cousin Al as Santa with his first Christmas present for my son

Me and my gal

Battle House at the Sun City Motel.
Your author is in the front row on the right.

I might have made that foul shot.

Our wedding day!

Sweet Sue singing at our wedding

I'm sitting in for the drummer at our wedding.

Tina and my mom in our backyard

Mom and Dad with their grandkids, Liz and Rob

The PS 215 schoolyard

PS 215 reunion with former alumni hosted by Brandon Steiner

PS 215's Mr. Kerper and Mr. Foti

Battle House reunion 2023 in Tampa.
I'm in the back row second to the right.

My PS 215 buddies, Joe and Richie.
We have been friends for over sixty years!

Glenn Brown, my old pal from Gravesend and I recently had lunch at our favorite Brooklyn pizza place. We've been friends since we were twelve.

About the Author

Tom Grippa was born and raised in Brooklyn, New York, as you can probably guess by the title of this book. This memoir of his early life, from 1952 to 1979, is his first book.

After graduating from Brooklyn College, he started his career as a commercial banker at First National City Bank (now known as Citibank) on February 14, 1977. He spent forty-one years working in different organizations and capacities within the financial services industry. When banking laws changed in 1999, allowing banks to offer a wider range of services, he added health and life insurance agent and registered stockbroker to his financial services résumé. He retired on February 2, 2018, from Signature Bank as a Group Director, Senior Vice President. His banking career started on Valentine's Day and ended on Groundhog Day.

Tom served honorably in the New York Army National Guard from 1972 to 1978. His home base was the Marcy Avenue Armory in Brooklyn, New York. His active service duty time included stops at Fort Dix, New Jersey, Fort Gordon, Georgia, Fort Bragg, North Carolina, Fort Drum, and Camp Smith in New York. He left that branch of the service with a rank of Specialist 4th class. He trained as a Tactical Wire Operations Specialist, Wire Systems Installer, and Company Clerk.

He has been married to his wife, Tina, for forty-five years. They have a daughter, son, and three grandchildren. He and his wife Tina reside in Eastern Pennsylvania near their daughter, son-in-law, and two grandchildren. He visits Forest Hills, New York, regularly, to see his son and grandson. Those trips usually include excursions to Long Island to see family members and friends.

On many occasions during his travels back to New York, Tom makes sure to take a detour through Brooklyn, which still holds a special place in his heart. It still has the best Italian bakeries and pizzerias in the country.

www.ingramcontent.com/pod-product-compliance
Lightning Source LLC
LaVergne TN
LVHW020926090426
835512LV00020B/3232